# All Cracked Up

Patsy Clairmont

THOMAS NELSON
*Since 1798*

Published in Nashville, Tennessee, by Thomas Nelson. Thomas Nelson is a registered trademark of Thomas Nelson, Inc.

All Scripture quotations, unless otherwise indicated, are taken from The New King James Version (NKJV®), 1979, 1980, 1982, Thomas Nelson, Inc. Publishers. Other Scripture quotations are taken from the following: The King James Version of the Bible (KJV). *The Message* (MSG), © 1993, 1994, 1995, 1996, 2000, 2001, 2002. Used by permission of NavPress Publishing Group. All rights reserved.

978-1-4002-7805-3 (TP)

**Library of Congress Cataloging-in-Publication Data**

Clairmont, Patsy.
All cracked up / Patsy Clairmont.
p. cm.
Includes index.
ISBN 978-0-8499-0047-1 (HC)
1. Christian women—Religious life. I. Title.
BV4527.C5325 2006
248.8'43—dc22

2005035029

*Printed in the United States of America*

*To my "Porch Pals"—*
*Nicole Johnson, Marilyn Meberg, Luci Swindoll, Sheila Walsh, and Thelma Wells—and the president of Women of Faith, Mary Graham, who make it a habit to shout their support, even when I'm all cracked up*

# Contents



## Part 1
## Cracked Pots

*Glass, china and reputation are easily cracked,*

*and never well mended.*

**—Benjamin Franklin**

## Part 2
## Wisecrackers

*We can learn much from wise words,*

*little from wisecracks, and less from wise guys.*

—William Arthur Ward

## Part 3
## Going Crackers

*Change, when it comes, cracks everything open.*

—Dorothy Allison

# Special Thanks

*I must thank two gifted friends for their involvement with this project:*

*Janet Grant, everything you touch is better.*
*Leslie Hurt, I love your passion for learning.*

*And thank you to my new friend Carolyn Denny, who walks her talk with grace and style.*

# 1

# All Cracked Up

OK, not funny! I don't know who spun the dial on my internal compass, but I'm not laughing. I just came from the mall, where I misplaced my car in the parking lot; and then, after finding it, I immediately got lost, detouring through three strip malls before careening (not purposely) onto the correct road headed for home. No, there are no strip malls on the way to my house. And no, the mall is not in another town. And yes, I had been there many times.

I've spent my whole life looking for where I belong. Well, not my *whole* life, since I spent my younger years following whomever was headed somewhere—anywhere—until I started to have more of a sense of self.

As I became a tad more certain of who I was, I became a little less certain of others' choices. This process is called "growing a brain," and from the best I can tell, it takes at least half a century, perhaps a little longer. It seems our brains have networks of hairline fractures through which brain cells trickle out and fog and pollution seep in.

So my advice is for us to Spackle. "Spackle" sounds a lot like "sparkle" minus the glitz. It's a gluelike substance meant to fill in fractures—*voila!* Brain gunk. We put gunk on our hair, so why not our brains?

Actually, all gunk aside, what I've learned thus far in life (besides never travel alone) is that my internal compass isn't the only thing broken. We also have obvious fissures of the heart, like fractured relationships, weakening moral fiber, and religious disillusionment. I wonder if Spackle comes in vats?

Actually, that's where our Redeemer comes in. We need someone who can fix broken hearts, Spackle our perspective, and even give us a reason to laugh. God sent Jesus as a Redeemer to do just that—to redeem the shards of our lives and create a stained-glass perspective. When we realize we're broken and acknowledge Jesus as our Redeemer, then the crushing blows of life do not destroy us; instead, we see through our repaired viewing place "the goodness of the LORD in the land of the living" (Psalm 27:13). Then we live with hope, we dance more often, we laugh more deeply, and we are not taken by surprise by the fact that life is all cracked up.

I don't have easy answers for the hardships of life, but I'd tell you if I did. Of course, I realize an old lady who wanders around a parking lot calling out to her PT Cruiser, "Oh, Babycakes!" is brain-cell suspect or at least a prime candidate for "the home."

In the pages ahead, we will look at some of our heart fractures and see reasons to crack up laughing. The topics are varied, but each chapter is tied to the next by one strand: cracks. I've included questions to tuck in your heart or to share in a group. The chapters will be short, because I can't think in a straight line very long before wandering off to the mall.

I've divided this project into three parts: *things* ("Cracked Pots"), *people* ("Wisecrackers"), and *changes* ("Going Crackers"). I created these parts because I need logical order to stay on track and not trot where rabbits scurry. Also, I've found these three areas fray my last nerve, stretch my reserves, and vie for my focus, strength, and attention.

First, I've included *things*, because things regularly crack in our lives. Just think about how much time you spend repairing all the stuff you've gathered around you. In the chapters ahead, we will investigate how damaged goods become prized possessions, how fractures become highlights, and how cracks can actually add value. As we will see in the pages ahead, "broken" doesn't have to mean "unusable." In fact, our brokenness can be the vibrancy that makes us even more valuable. I love that.

Second, I've included *people* because—well, I am one, and also because they play a featured part in our lives. People build us, bamboozle us, baffle us, and bless us. Sometimes we can't live with them, and we certainly weren't designed to live without them.

Finally, I've included *change*, because it is the door to discovery. We weren't meant to be static but dynamic, and dynamics are charged by change. Yet change is not always an easy door to walk through, whether it's a crack in the door or the door's wide open. So let's walk through that door together.

As you turn the pages through these stories about things, people, and change, I'd love it if you laugh yourself silly and then go live yourself sane. I've found that even a lively chuckle helps make room for a fresh run at life. So if you're in a good place, come giggle till you jiggle. If you're feeling debilitated, come be tenderly heartened. And if you're somewhere in between, then be prepared—we'll be laughing one minute and sighing the next.

It's a mystery how life can be both fun and fractured. But there it is—all cracked up.

# Part 1

# Cracked Pots

*Glass, china and reputation are easily cracked, and never well mended.*

—Benjamin Franklin

## 2

# Brain Fractures

Know what fractures my brain? Numbers. Somehow they just don't tally for me.

It makes me nervous just saying the word *math*. Or worse yet, *algebra*. (Isn't that a type of undergarment?) Or what about *metric*? Eek!

Any numerical word can cause me to hyperventilate. Numbers just don't stick in my brain, not even with superglue. When someone asks me how old I am and I pause before answering, it may seem like I'm in denial; but truth is, I forget. And I hate to say, "Just a second; I'll check my driver's license." Or, "Wait a minute; I'll ask my kids." Nor do I feel comfortable just confessing, "I don't know," for fear they'll call the Old-Age Patrol.

Age is so fluctuating. I mean, it just keeps switching on me. If my age would stay the same for, say, a decade at a time, it would really help.

Once, I told a fellow who had asked my age that I was 85-43. He stared at me like he thought my cranium was cracked.

My mind was intact; it was my numbers I had flip-flopped. I had inadvertently given him my address . . . from three houses ago. Well, at least I didn't give him my Social Security number.

I blame my number dilemma on the multiplication tables. They messed me up. Honestly, I was doing fine in school until I had to multiply. Adding and subtracting were fairly friendly, but multiplying was hostile from the get-go. I spent untold hours being drilled on the multiplication tables via flash cards by my more-than-determined mom. I promise you, even using a high-powered drill (and my mom was), I still can't say my nines.

And if multiplying weren't bad enough, then I had to learn fractions. I say, if it's a fraction of anything, why bother? Get over the small stuff. Just dust it away and keep moving. That way, nobody gets hurt.

Have you noticed how many numbers we are required to know to function in society? Sooner rather than later, folks ask us either to take a number, number off, or spout a list of digits the breadth of North America: address, zip code, telephone number, age, date of birth, Social Security number, P.O. box, license plate number, driver's license number, hotel room, the time, combination lock, today's date, families' dates of birth, PIN number, security system code, shoe size, frequent-flyer number, height, and weight (like I'm telling that!). No wonder people *punch* time clocks—they're angry that they've had to deal with one more set of numbers!

When I grew up, I thought I wanted to punch a clock as a bookstore owner, but God protected my prospective customers and me because he knew I would need to know more than how to read a book—I'd have to know how to keep the books. I can't even handle the cash register, much less balance columns of figures. My idea of balancing books is holding one in each hand. And inventory? Just call in the white coats. My eyes glaze over when I see shelves laden with anything that I might have to compute.

For years I wasn't certain God meant for us to mess with numbers, but then I remembered Noah, who had to count the animals. Not a job I'd want. I've seen those pictures of all the animals agreeably lining up and filing aboard the ark, but I don't buy it. I think they were squirming, nipping, bucking, and hiding. I think loading that ark put stretch marks on Noah's grace. Have you ever tried to count rooting pigs, hysterical hyenas, or hot-flashing penguins? And who can keep track of numbers with trumpeting elephants, screeching monkeys, and squawking parrots? Don't you just know the donkeys sat down on the gangplank more than once and refused to budge, jamming the count? No, make me a greeter at Wal-Mart where I nod and "Howdy-ya-do?" the folks coming aboard, but don't make me calculate anything.

The Lord has instructed us to "number our days." I am on day 21,763. Or so I think. No one is here to check my math. I wouldn't even try to figure it out, except the Lord asks me to, so it must be important. Maybe it's a type of righteous reality check. Sort of a "Here's what I've given you thus far, what have you done with it?"

Why don't you grab a pencil and jot in the margin what day you're on? Go ahead; it's all right to use your calculator.

My husband, Les, has a calculator for a brain—he could

have been Noah. He not only clearly remembers my age and weight, but he also remembers his army number from forty years ago. I think that's rude.

He can add up figures in his head faster than I can find a pencil and paper. How I, a numberless woman, married Les, a statistical mastermind, is beyond me. I used to think he rattled off digits just to annoy me. Now, after years of being mathematically humiliated, I realize he and his amazing mind are gifts to complete me. I could have saved myself years of frustration if I'd have grasped that right off the bat.

OK, let's see . . . I met Les in 1960, which was 45 years ago when I was 15 . . . I married him 43 years ago when I was 17, but he went to Germany for 18 months, so that, deducted from 43, leaves . . . oh, never mind!

*Lord, we're so aware of what we can't do that sometimes we forget to thank you for what we can do. So thank you for making us the way you have. And thank you for those you've placed in our lives to fill gaps. Help us to graciously step in the gap for others. And we will be mindful to number our days. Amen.*

## Cracked-Up Questions

**What abilities come naturally to you?**

**How do you value your abilities?**

**Is your age an issue for you? Why?**

**Who helps complete you? How?**

# 3

# Heat Index

Texas getteth hot.

I know that's not a news flash for most of the country, but unless you've been in Texas in August, you can't appreciate the sweat it takes even to type that opening statement. The Lone Star State knows how to do heat.

How hot is it? The women here don't wear pantyhose for fear their hose will melt down their legs and puddle in their shoes. I noticed that the ants wear sunscreen, and the birds have blisters on their beaks and crunch sun-fried worms. Why, just the other day, I saw an armadillo trying to cool off by ambling through a carwash. OK, OK, maybe not—but I promise you, it's hot.

So with desert-type heat and watering restrictions, you can imagine that attempting to flower up the parched summer landscape is no easy task. But in northeast Texas, they have a flouncy, bouncy girlfriend who struts her stuff right down the boulevard, petticoats and all, and shakes her lovely branches at the sun. Her name is Myrtle.

Crepe Myrtle is a flowering shrub that provides an oasis of color in this state's beige setting. It grows up to thirty-five feet and has branches that spew forth pink, white, mauve, or lavender blossoms throughout the summer.

God bless you, Myrtle. For while everything else is shriveling up, Myrtle is shouting hallelujahs. Her ability to stretch her blossoms toward heaven as well as bend her branches to kiss the earth despite the sizzling heat makes her a landscaper's dream.

Of course, as in all of life, Myrtle has a couple of "issues." She is susceptible to mold, and she is frequently the victim of overzealous pruning. Sometimes backyard gardeners think that a healthy pruning will bring more blossoms the following year, when in actuality, Myrtle doesn't bear up well through the winter if someone's been hacking on her in the fall. (I know how you feel, honey.) She needs her inner strength not only to endure the colder months but also to make preparations for her next showy summer's wardrobe.

I can learn from Myrtle. Even though I've grown to my full stature of five feet and will never reach her heights, she's full of lessons. To bear up beautifully like Myrtle when life heats up and dries out is scriptural. The prophet Jeremiah puts it this way: "For [she] shall be like a tree . . . And will not be anxious in the year of drought, nor will cease from yielding fruit" (Jeremiah 17:8).

In my estimation, it's far more difficult to bear anything, much less clusters of flowers, when we feel hot and dry. Yesterday in Texas, it was 102 degrees. Goodness, in my home state of Michigan, that's not a temperature; that's a basketball score. But in Texas, it's called "daytime." The weatherman said no rain is in sight in the long-range forecast. Just hearing that caused the moisture in my soul to evaporate.

(I have to add this update. The night after I wrote the above, we did have rain, and the temperature cooled down to 101. Thought you should know.)

Here's what stands out to me about Myrtle: she bears fruit with grace under pressure. I personally droop when not watered. In fact, I was diagnosed several years ago with osteoporosis—brittle bones—so I understand being dry and drooping. Osteo makes you think twice before jumping over high buildings in a single bound. Actually, it's all I can do not to trip on curbs. Also, I no longer wear shoes that don't feel secure. (Oh my, I am my mother.) And I have to remind myself constantly to stand up straight because I'm definitely tilting toward terra firma.

I wonder if Myrtle has ever met my well-watered friend Ginny? They sure act alike. Ginny has flourished even through extended droughts that would have wilted most. The death of dear ones, a life-altering accident, a five-engine house fire, a divorce (not hers), and a devastating illness have left her family in a long dry spell.

Yet Ginny hasn't stopped flowering. Some of her branches have bent and kissed the earth in weeping, but even her tears served to bring forth more blossoms. I've watched her repeatedly reach for God's truths to water her mind and replenish her roots (and I'm not talking hair). And even when a few overzealous pruners showed up on her landscape, she held her own. Ginny laughs often, loves deliberately, and lives abundantly. She is my hallelujah friend.

Ginny and Myrtle have been good examples for me because, left on my own, my tendency is to laugh sporadically, love selectively, and live reluctantly. What a narrow existence that leaves! So when life heats up and I'm tempted to wilt and droop, I think of my friends and choose instead to shout hallelujahs and stretch my arms to heaven, knowing that even in the dry seasons I can bloom and bear fruit pleasing to the master Gardener.

*Lord, you designed the Myrtles and then placed them where they would do the most good. We believe the same about ourselves. Even if we never understand the droughts of our lives, may we continue to shout our hallelujahs to you. Thank you that your loving plans aren't just for a season, but you supply our needs throughout every season. Protect us from folks who want to prune us, lest they lop off a branch you designed to flourish. May we stand tall and bloom profusely. Amen.*

## Cracked-Up Questions

**How is your life's landscape? Flourishing? Parched?**

**What overzealous pruners have invaded your life?**

**Who are your hallelujah friends?**

**What "mold" issues are in your life?**

**Describe in one word for each how you live, laugh, and love.**

4

# Make a Splash

I'm a collector. I collect dust. I can't be trusted to collect anything else. I tend to . . . uh . . . overdo. I start on a collection, and I don't know when to stop. Take my teapots . . . no, really, take them. I have so many they cause me to brew and spout.

I love the shapes of teapots, and I appreciate their hospitable reputation. They promote friendship, conversations, gentility, comfort, and well-being. But the truth is, too many of anything is just too many. I have fat pots, squat pots, tall pots, silver pots, animal-shaped pots, spiffy new pots, and family heirlooms. Some of my teapots you can't even put hot water in!

Somewhere along the teapot route, I slid down the Milky Way and began to collect milk bottles. My dad was a Sealtest milkman when I was growing up, so I decided to collect bottles, but only from that company—that way, the collection wouldn't get out of hand. Oh, sure. Do you know how many bottles are roaming the earth from that company? Bazillions. My house began to look like a creamery. All I lacked was a herd of Holsteins and a mound of hay. Why, I had baskets, crates, and cupboards crammed with half-pints, pints, quarts, half-gallons, and gallon jugs. Not to mention all my Sealtest paraphernalia (spoons, ice cream containers, rulers, bottle caps, booklets, signs, recipes).

The collection grew rapidly because my husband and I entered into an unspoken yet obvious competition. We would arrive at an antique store and nonchalantly saunter down separate aisles on opposite sides of the store. Then we would pick up a galloping pace. A short time later, with beads of sweat glowing on our brows, we would meet up, breathless, at the checkout counter. Each of us would be clutching Sealtest bottles to our breasts like Midas's gold. And if one of us arrived wearing a sly grin that dripped off the side of our mouth like melted ice cream, it meant we had found a bottle that wasn't in the collection yet. We would try to act unimpressed with our find, but gloating is like bloating; it's hard to hide.

Then I switched spigots when, instead of collecting bottles, I gathered old water pitchers from hither and yon. I already had a couple of pitchers that had belonged to my grandmother and mom, and I thought I could use a few more. Well, by now you know what happened. Why, I could have filled my myriad pitchers with enough liquid to water the Sahara. OK, maybe not the Sahara, but certainly all the camels in Tibet. (Do they have camels there?) Well, anyway, I had enough to fill Jacob's well at Samaria. Where's that, you inquire? Thank you, I was hoping you would ask. Here, jot down the address. There may be times you feel parched, and you'll want to read this account: John 4:5–30.

In this Bible story, we meet a woman drawing water from a well. She had balanced a pitcher on her head all the way from her village, but instead of simply filling her water vessel and heading back home as she had a thousand times before, she encountered a man sitting near the well who forever changed her life.

The man asked her for a drink. Sounds simple enough, right? Nothing life-changing about that. In fact, it just sounds like more work for her. But then he said that God could give her living water, and she would never thirst again. Now that statement gained her attention.

*Never thirst again.* Who wouldn't want that kind of water? Who wouldn't want the burden of daily responsibility lifted off her head, back, and shoulders—much less have the ache of her thirst relieved?

Instead of giving the water to the woman, Jesus asked her to call her husband and have him join her. She then confessed to Christ that she had no husband. To which he replied, "You have well said, 'I have no husband,' for you have had five husbands, and the one whom you now have is not your husband; in that you spoke truly" (vv. 17–18).

Well, would you look at that? The Samaritan woman was a collector too. Five husbands . . . wow! And now she had a live-in. It often seems collections cost us more than we meant to pay. I think the woman at the well would quote the great theologian who said, "Too many of anything is just too many." Oh, wait, that was me. Never mind.

The Samaritan woman was searching for something that would quench her longing and perhaps fill her loneliness, but she obviously was having trouble finding it. No wonder Jesus's offer of living water captured her attention—and the empty cistern of her heart. We know it did, because she couldn't wait to tell others about him. That's how it is when our heart begins to overflow; we have enough to offer others.

The woman at the well couldn't believe that Jesus would speak to her. Have you ever felt that way? I have. I know my blatant inadequacies and how I've tried to meet my own needs by drinking from man-made wells where the water didn't satisfy. Yet Christ knew everything the Samaritan woman had done (v. 30), and he still spoke to her. And, knowing everything about us, he speaks to you and to me. Jesus's offer to give us living water is as clear and pure now as it was that day at Jacob's well. He doesn't withhold his offer because we are empty, broken, or contaminated. In fact, he understands our condition, and he comes with the cleansing water of forgiveness, inviting us to drink and be forever refreshed.

Are you thirsty?

*Lord, nothing we can gather on earth will satisfy our thirst; it's too great, too deep, too constant. Ladle to our lips your living water, that we might never seek fresh water again in the polluted pools of our own making. And may we go forth and splash the world. Amen.*

## Cracked-Up Questions

What do you collect?

Are you in competition with anyone? Who? Why?

Had a case of gloat lately? What over?

What daily responsibilities weigh you down?

Describe the condition of your heart's well.

Have you ever drunk deeply from the living water and experienced Christ's forgiveness for your sins? If so, when? If not, why not?

## 5

# Patsy Want a Cracker?

One of my favorite lunches is a bowl of soup with a pile of crackers. Maybe because that was a regular on the menu when I was growing up. My mom always served me chicken noodle soup and crackers when I was sick—the very definition of comfort food. And as far back as I can remember, soda crackers were a staple in my grandmother's menu.

I'm not the only child who grew up with crackers. These salty treats have existed since 1792. In that year, John Pearson, who lived close to the sea in Newburyport, Massachusetts, made a crackerlike bread from flour and water. He called it "pilot bread," and sailors took an immediate liking to it because it had a long shelf life. That's when it also became known as "hardtack" or "sea biscuit." Which, I guess, means the horse Sea Biscuit was aptly named, since he, too, wasn't anything fancy, but folks took a real liking to him.

Enthusiasm for the cracker grew in 1801 when another Massachusetts baker, Josiah Bent, burned a batch of biscuits in his brick oven. Those singed babies made a crackling noise when he pulled them out of the oven, which inspired their current name. Bent, being a pecuniary kind of guy, decided to sell the crackers as snack food. His customers loved those burnt offerings, and by 1810, most folks in the Boston area were adding crackers to their grocery lists.

Just think: all those culinary failures I've had could have ended up as an American staple if I'd just shown a little Yankee ingenuity. Why, I've burned plenty of things, including my potholder. And once I burned a skillet of chicken. Wait, did I say "burned"? I meant charred. It definitely crackled when we bit into it.

The Bible has its own cracker story. Manna is described as a small, round substance, which Moses proclaimed to be "the bread" God had provided for the Israelites in the wilderness. It appeared on the ground every morning, sort of like I find frost when I step out of the house on a cool winter morning. Manna is referred to as "the bread of heaven" (Psalm 105:40), which was literally true since it rained down from heaven as provision for the Israelites (see Exodus 16:4).

At first, the Hebrews were awed and grateful for this bounty from heaven. But after, say, a month or two of the same fare, this staple in their diet (which they ended up eating for every meal for forty years) began to wear a little thin. No wonder they pined for the leeks they had left behind in Egypt. The idea of finding milk and honey in the Promised Land made them salivate.

The Israelites named this mysterious bread "manna," which in Hebrew means "What is it?" My family often asks that question when I present the evening meal to them.

Don't I know what they mean! Frequently when God places manna on my plate, I have one of two responses, both of which sound an awful lot like the Israelites' whining. I might take a look at the Lord's latest "gift" and say, "What's this? God, I don't remember asking for patience. So why is the driver in front of me dawdling like we're in a parade? Not to mention his blinker's been on for a left-hand turn for the last four blocks."

Or I might give God a piece of my mind (as if I have any pieces to spare) when the fare is unchanging. "What's this? Lord, I think I've put up with the flu for long enough. Time for a change of venue, thank you very much."

I especially felt that way when Les and I took a rare trip together to celebrate our forty-first wedding anniversary. We decided to travel together on a Women of Faith Alaskan cruise and plunked down the extra cash to have a room with a big view. But as soon as we boarded, we realized we were both coming down with a bad case of the flu. While we were thankful we had a window to watch Alaska slip past us, our toes seldom touched the Alaskan tundra, and the luscious meals held no interest for us. The staple in our diet that week was—you guessed it!—crackers.

So, yes, manna comes in forms we don't always appreciate. I regularly need to be reminded that manna is provision from God, sustenance for my soul to be eaten with gratefulness. Rather than responding to the item on my platter with the question, "What is it?" I would be better off saying, "Well, now, what's this?"

Patsy want a cracker? Yes, Lord. Thanks.

*Bread of Life, thank you for providing for me all that I require in life—not only ample supplies of food but also sustenance for my heart and soul. Thank you that you supply manna even when I don't always graciously receive it. Help me to remember, as your heavenly gifts float into my life, that they come from your good hand. And help me to receive them as coming from you.*

## Cracked-Up Questions

**What's your favorite memory of crackers?**

**Recall a time you received something as a pleasant surprise from God.**

**Can you remember a time you grew tired of the "manna" God was providing for you?**

**What about a time you wanted a different gift from the one God gave you?**

**What "manna" is in your life today?**

**Do you think a change of attitude might be in order as you consider your "manna"? What's a good way to start?**

## 6

# The Fragrance of Roses

*You love the roses—so do I. I wish*
*The sky would rain down roses, as they rain*
*From off the shaken bush. Why will it not?*
*Then all the valley would be pink and white*
*And soft to tread on. They would fall as light*
*As feathers, smelling sweet and it would be*
*Like sleeping and yet waking, all at once.*
—George Eliot

Ah, the rose, the flower of romance. A rose's stunning beauty and wafting perfume have won the hearts of many lovers, not to mention the fervor of many gardeners. A fistful of American Beauties can cause a gal's heart to tremble and cause a gardener to shout for joy.

My husband loves to bring me surprises, and he's good at it. Oh, there have been a few gifts that I wish he'd have skipped (like the horsehair purse—*ah-choo*!), but generally speaking, Les courts me well.

On a recent birthday, he presented me with one long-stemmed rose for every year I have been alive. Oh my, talk about an extravagant reality check; it looked like the Rose Parade wedged in a vase.

One man, Charles H. Pond, still gave roses to his wife, Elizabeth, after her earthly departure. Now that's romantic. Not for her, of course—but for us. You see, upon his passing, the Hartford, Connecticut, industrialist-statesman left land to the city for a horticultural endeavor to be named after his wife. Isn't that dear? How lovely to be remembered in such a rosy way.

Today the one-hundred-acre Elizabeth Park is the oldest municipally operated rose garden in the country and is known throughout the world. The floral offering has two-and-a-half acres designated in remembrance of Elizabeth, with more than fifteen thousand bushes touting eight hundred rose varieties.

Fifteen thousand bushes—wow! That must take a herd of gardeners to oversee. They may want to check with Confucius; I understand he had a six-hundred-book library on how to care for the rose. Now *that's* a passionate gardener!

Emma Goldman put her floral passion this way: "I'd rather have roses on my table than diamonds on my neck." Now, Emma, we need to talk. Always keep your options open, honey, and maybe, just maybe, you could have both.

I personally am a looker at roses rather than, say, a handler or a sniffer. No, I'm definitely not a sniffer. My allergies just can't take up-close-and-personal encounters with flowers. So I stand a leap away and applaud their beauty from afar. As you might imagine, with my oversensitive nose, I don't do potpourri either. I want to, but my itching eyes, drippy nose, and sneezing fits suggest otherwise. You should see me sprint through the perfume sections of department stores, hanky over mouth, nostrils quivering, as I turn blue from holding my breath. Quite lovely, I must say.

Historians believe that potpourri was first used in the twelfth century to improve the stuffy air in dank castle rooms. It also was used to freshen ladies' petticoats, since there was a shortage of Laundromats in Ye Old City Square. In the days of knights and ladies, baskets were filled with rose heads and other flowers, some crushed petals, perhaps some cedar tips, and some aromatic spices. Once that mixture had seasoned, the baskets of fragrance were strategically placed throughout the castle.

I've also heard that Cleopatra's palace floors were covered with delicate rose petals. Imagine wading ankle-deep in the rose's soft fragrance. How feminine—and how extravagant.

I'm impressed with the rose because of its fruitful existence. It begins as a bud, which has a beauty all its own; gracefully unfolds into velvet overlays; and then, with its last breath, when crushed, it leaves a heady fragrance and drips precious oil. OK, there is the thorn issue, but in the overall scope of flower life, the rose is the reigning queen.

As we consider the beauty and grace of the rose, we're not surprised to discover that Jesus is called the Rose of Sharon. He was born a bud of a babe in a manger; his beauty unfolded before others with each humble step he took; and in his last breaths on earth, with thorns pressed into his head, after being crushed by our sins, he shed precious drops of his blood and released a forever fragrance of love. In the overall scope of our life, Christ is our coming King.

That sacrifice, Christ's broken body, now calls us to receive the crushing blows of life as a way for his fragrance to be released through us. I had never thought of our crushed and drooping lives as having the potential of becoming a holy potpourri. Take a shattered heart, mix with a crushed spirit, intermingle with Christ's oil of mercy, stir with his healing touch, and season with divine love. Once our redeemed pain is liberally placed around, his fragrance will waft down the corridors of this old musty castle of a world.

*You may break; you may shatter the vase, if you will.*
*But the scent of roses will hang round it still.*
—Thomas More

*Lord God, may the sweet scent of Christ be upon us so that others might be wooed into the garden of your presence. Remove the thorns of offense from us that inflict pain and that distance those whom you love. May we walk through others' lives as gingerly as if we were tiptoeing through rose petals. Thank you for being our gardener, for we are in need of your tender care. Amen.*

## Cracked-Up Questions

**What are your favorite fragrances?**

**What do you think the fragrance of Christ smells like?**

**When crushed, what fragrance do you emit?**

**How can you release Christ's oil of mercy?**

**How has your pain been redeemed?**

## Just for FuN

# Christmas Crackers

Christmas at our house is a sparkly event. Each year, Les seems to add another tree to our collection. We now have seven trees scattered throughout the house, each dancing with Christmas decorations.

While I love our festive trees, a highlight of the holiday is Christmas dinner. Setting the table is my specialty; cooking the food is not. I cook, but it's the decorating that keeps folks coming back . . . trust me. My plum pudding is plum awful.

One year, a friend sent me a package of Christmas crackers, which became our place-setting gifts. If you've never seen a Christmas cracker, it's like a party in a tube. Or in my vernacular, they're "the small bang theory."

The cardboard tube is about six inches long and festooned with brightly decorated paper with a twist at the end, making it look like an oversized candy wrapper. When you pull on the wrapper, it pops open, accompanied with a small bang. Out cascades a colored paper hat, a small toy, and a scrap of paper containing a joke or piece of trivia.

Suddenly all formality vanishes and a party spirit pops into place. Donning their hats, guests read from their bits of paper and show off their toys. It's a standing joke in our family that the toy will be awful, the hat will be hideous, and the joke on the paper will be lame, all of which for some reason only adds to the laughter at the table.

The "crackle" portion of the tube was added when Tom Smith, the Christmas cracker's inventor, put a log on the fire in 1847, and the log crackled. He decided that a bit of a bang when the tube was cracked open would be just the ticket he was looking for to increase sales. And indeed it was, especially in Britain where the crackers are an integral part of the celebration.

My grandson Noah (two and a half years old) is also a celebration with a pop. I lovingly call him Cannonball because he doesn't enter a room; he literally casts himself into one's presence with great velocity. Noah's specialty is his headlong, anything-goes attitude, and he has a sparkly smile that could illuminate every holiday tree I own.

Recently, my son Jason took Noah to his tumbling class. The teacher instructed the class to go to another room, but Noah was busy turning head over heels on a mat, so the teacher called to him, "C'mon, Demolition Man."

Yep, it doesn't take long to spot a boy full of crackle. Last year, Noah, just a toddler, was fascinated with the ornaments on our entry tree. Before we could stop him, he reached out and bit into one of the red glass balls. Gratefully, he didn't cut himself, but the ball was definitely all cracked up.

The next time you want to add bang to a celebration, I recommend gift crackers—or borrow a crackle boy if you don't have one . . . just for fun!

# 7

# Cody the Canine Crackup

You know what cracks me up? I have a grand-dog.

For many years, I could hardly wait to become a grandma; but trust me, I never considered the possibility of having a grand-dog. Nor had I ever been introduced to a Jack Russell terrier (alias Wacky Raucous Scarier) until our son's dog, Cody, came for an unescorted, extended visit. I didn't remember sending an invitation, but sure enough, he arrived at my doorstep wagging his tail behind him.

Did I say behind him? Let me restate that. Cody's breed, when on the defensive, points its tail skyward and vibrates it like a Geiger counter needle detecting a find. And while initially all that tail gyrating appears to be a friendly gesture, one soon realizes that Cody is announcing that your presence profoundly annoys him. To support his threatening effort, he adds a growling murmur, suggesting that the offending party should "back away now."

After just a short time together, Cody and I needed a

therapist because our dysfunctional relationship was wearing me down. I tried to sway Cody's aggressive behavior with doggie treats, but he was unimpressed. I even fixed him an egg—with melted cheese, mind you. After I served it to him, he growled at me for standing too close to his dish.

Then I bought him a toy lion, to which he seemed to respond gleefully. But within three minutes, he dropped the now maneless lion at my feet. When I looked down, I saw he had also ripped off the lion's nose and pulled out the stuffing from the open cavity. Now, I could be reading into this, but this gesture felt like a direct warning: "Watch out, Grandma. You're next!"

Les and I usually retire around midnight. Customarily, Les slips into bed a few minutes before I arrive. (Girls have beauty regimens, you know.)

But A.C. (After Cody), when I would step out of the bathroom and head for my side of the bed, I would meet opposition. Cody had bonded with Les and had apparently decided that only one of us could sleep near him, and it wasn't going to be me. With tail twitching and head down, Cody served up his deepest murmurings. Les had to repeatedly rebuff his guard dog so I could clamber into my own bed. The battle was on, and Cody was about to find out I could snarl too.

Early one morning, Cody indicated by ecstatic leaps that he wanted to go outside. So I told Les I would do the honors. I dragged my body to an upright position, grabbed my housecoat, slid into my slippers, and headed for the front door. In hindsight (no pun intended), I realized Cody wasn't indicating he needed to go outside. He was celebrating that he already had gone . . . inside. And what I first thought was unfeigned enthusiasm for me was actually his lauding his achievement in my face, or more accurately, on my foot.

The truth of his dastardly deed sunk in as I submerged my foot in a large, ahem, "deposit" that Cody had left on the hall rug. Not realizing I was foot-first in fresh deposit, I stepped onto the hardwood floor and slid three feet to the front door. I howled as I slid, but I wasn't laughing. I'm not that enthused about mornings to begin with, so when you add stepping in dog doo to waking up at the crack of dawn, the statistical probability of me having a good day is not promising. (I'd tell you the exact numbers, but I've forgotten them already.)

Les, hearing my howl, came on the run, thinking Cody was once again threatening me. Instead, Les found me—miniature, gray-haired, and on all fours—growling at that fifteen-pound Oscar Mayer gonna-be.

Now don't get me wrong; Cody is cute. In fact, he's darling. But he certainly isn't cuddly, and he would never win Mr. Congeniality. He's deliberately antisocial and purposes to maintain a short dance card.

Cody does have his moments when he will bound into my office carrying a toy and want to play, but his idea of "play" is for me to chase him around the house. Now, for the sake of relationship, I try. But quite honestly, I'm too cotton-pickin' old to be sprinting around couches, chairs, and tables in pursuit of a three-year-old puppy. Besides, my house can't take the jarring that my bounding creates; and for some reason, I don't take corners as gracefully as I once did.

When our grandchildren come over, Cody gets a full

workout. But he is the instigator. Not long after our grandsons bebop through my door, great shouts of glee reach the house rafters as riotous racers speed through the halls. Cody, who's always in the lead, has one of the children's toys firmly gripped between his molars, and he's grinning.

Cody loves stuffed animals, small plastic toys, and shoes. His goal is to gnaw them into oblivion. So far, he has shortened the neck of a giraffe, de-trunked two elephants, and put serious doubt in a stuffed lion that he is truly king. One thing I know for sure: Noah wouldn't have wanted Cody on the ark.

But Noah can't have him anyway—I don't give away family. Grandmas are like that, you know. I'm committed to this growling, gnawing, oversized gerbil of a dog . . . who makes me laugh daily. Unbridled enthusiasm is endearing, and Cody's breed, like Superman, can leap tall buildings in a single bound.

When I think about it, what are a few altered belongings between family members? And what clan doesn't have a few growlers in its midst? Besides, who but Cody would bound to the door each time I come home, genuinely glad to see me (at least initially)?

There's nothing like family!

*Lord, thank you for your marvelous creations, full of energy and antics. Your creativity amazes and delights us. You knew some of us would need what pets have to offer. May we repay them with kindness. Amen.*

## Cracked-Up Questions

How do you respond to unexpected guests in your life?

Who in your house growls? Why?

How can you find more grace-space when things aren't going your way?

Are you easily annoyed?

Do you see the best in people?

Who in your world greets you with unbridled enthusiasm?

# 8

# It's a Shoe-In

What's more painful than breaking in a new pair of shoes? No, don't tell me; my blisters are screaming so loud I couldn't hear you anyway.

I love shoes . . . usually. Not right this minute, but once I've broken in these size 5½ loafers to feel like 6s, I'll be back into touting their design.

My last pair of 6s kept tripping me up. It's embarrassing to be walking along and stumble over wads of air. I can't tell you how many times I've tripped and then looked back on my path, only to see nothing was there to trip on. Not a cotton-pickin' thing. I decided my shoes must be too long, causing me to trip on the shoe tips, so I bought a smaller size. OK, call me cracked up. Now it takes a can opener and a chisel to jam my foot inside my shoes. I no longer trip; in fact, I can hardly walk. Is there such a thing as a size 5¾?

Shoes have come a long way from being simple coverings for our weary feet to being collectibles for a woman's wardrobe. Generally, men aren't as smitten with shoes. My husband owns two pairs. He purchased the second pair on a whim. Even retailers are aware of ladies' obsession—I mean, ahem, keen interest—in their foot dressings.

Recently, a major chocolate company teamed up with a high-fashion shoe designer. Now that's a genius marketing strategy (so long as they don't start making chocolate shoes). The companies waged a national contest in which the top prize included luscious chocolates and thousands of dollars in shoes. The gal who won just happened to be from a family with two other sisters and a mom, and—get this!—they all wore the same size shoe. What fun! I bet as I write they are all lining up at her closet door. Yep, give us gals a box of truffles and a pair of sparkly flip-flops, and you've won our attention if not our admiration.

I just checked eBay, and it listed 36,900 pairs of shoes for sale. Imagine that. I typed in my size, and they offered four pages of shoe choices. From mules, to boots, to heels, to wedges, to loafers, to tennis shoes, to sandals, we girls sure like to walk in style. As a matter of fact, North Americans spend almost $18 billion a year on footwear—and you can guess that women are making major contributions to that statistic.

The Bible speaks of footwear, but even more of our walk. Especially our walk. Genesis mentions Adam and Eve's barefoot walk with the Lord in the cool of the evening. The Bible closes with the dramatic account of John's vision of the Son of Man in which his feet are like fine brass. Scripture reminds us of the importance of where we walk, how we walk, and with whom we walk.

Consider Ruth, who, during her time of stepping through

the valley of the shadow of death when her husband died, chose to follow her mother-in-law to a new land—a land where Ruth would know no one, look different, and spend her days serving her broken and bitter mother-in-law. While that may sound like Ruth made a hasty choice, God intervened on her behalf and made provisions for her that would lead her into a loving marriage and even restore her mother-in-law's joy. I don't know about you, but I don't naturally rush to don the sandals of a servant, which is why Ruth's story is a good reminder.

Life is so textured, full of nubs like a bolt of tweed fabric, interesting and unpredictable. We are walking down a delightful path when, without warning, we find ourselves on a path we never would have chosen. Then our choice becomes whether we will trudge or high-step our way to the finish line.

Recently, two individuals who are exceptional high-steppers have been in the news. One was a young man who cut off his own arm to save his life after being pinned down by a rock on a remote mountainside. The other was a young girl who lost her arm in a shark attack while surfing. Both strong athletes were walking out their passions, but both now walk uncharted paths. They never could have expected such radical change. Yet, during television interviews, each of them has spoken of gratitude—not for their loss, but for their lives.

That impressed me. I can imagine the up-and-down emotions this young man and woman will experience as they attempt to live out of a happy heart despite days of phantom pain, physical limitations, and social implications. And I know that experiencing gratitude in the midst of tragedy is a breakthrough. It can take a long time—even with hiking boots—to push through the fog of our grief and to reach that gratitude pinnacle, which offers us another perspective . . . a view beyond our losses.

Loss opens a walkway to what really matters in life. It presses us to see and feel in ways we hadn't previously considered. And while loss doesn't seem like a friend, it often brings refining touches to our character. It can hone compassion toward others, it can move us beyond fear, it can help us to determine a clear-cut path, and it can deepen our dependence on God.

My tendency is to pull on track shoes and sprint in the opposite direction of loss, because it fractures dreams. But I am learning ever so slowly to lean into it and lift my heels.

*Lord, shod our feet with sandals of devotion toward you. It's easy in this life to lose our way. Give us courage to sprint in your direction. We look forward to the day when we shall sit at your holy feet. Amen.*

## Cracked-Up Questions

**If life were a pair of shoes,**
**how would you describe yours?**

**What sharp turn has your path taken?**

**Are servants' sandals part of your wardrobe?**
**How do you serve others?**

**Have your losses defined you or refined you?**

**Are you trudging or high-stepping in your**
**day-to-day existence? Why?**

# 9

# Words of Wisdom, Words of Whimsy

Want to crack open a book with me? I love books. I like old books that smell like my grandmother's trunk. I like new books with covers that crack with freshness, ones in which I'm the first to peruse the pristine pages. I like books that have copious notes in the margins so I can track other readers' thoughts. I applaud the added dimension of illustrations, because I'm a visual learner. I appreciate dog-eared and underlined volumes from friends and family members that help me to know that person better. And the fanciful tales in children's books fill my whimsy tank and encourage me to lighten up.

One of my favorite lighten-up gifts is a shopping spree at a bookstore. Recently, for my birthday, several friends gave me gift cards for a bookstore extravaganza. How fun is that!

Les and I often date at the bookstore. While he visits the

café, I browse the shelves. The books' colorful spines look like rows of Life Savers just waiting for me to savor their sweetness.

I don't have to buy armloads of books to be giddy, just one or two . . . OK, three or four . . . hand-selected choices. I enjoy a wide range of reading, although I tend to favor genres in spurts. Right now, I'm spurting fiction.

Fiction allows us to step out our front door and onto an island. Who doesn't want to do that? As I meet new people page after page and learn their ways, I then tag along to see the ramifications of their decisions. Often I leave a novel in a contemplative mood, ruminating over the cast of characters and their choices, which causes me to measure my own.

Right now I'm reading Charles Martin's *Wrapped in Rain* (WestBow, 2005), and I'm at rapt attention. He has a keen ability to take a reader inside the scenes of his story. Martin's pen is poignant, pensive, and profound.

I also enjoy autobiographies. I like knowing the inside scoop. It's fun reading other people's mail and seeing the difficulties they faced, the obstacles they've hurtled, and the heartbreak they've endured. Often someone's story leaves me feeling less alone and more able to bear up in the midst of my own unfolding saga.

I recently enjoyed reading *Salvage*, the autobiography of David Pierce (Theland, 2005). David's background captivates me, since his life is full of scallywags and daggers. He paints pictures of his childhood with wild strokes. His life reads like an adventure, verges on tragedy, and culminates in victory. It reminds me that every living person has a memorable story worthy of shouting from the rooftops.

One of my favorite books to investigate is the book of James. I'm aware that some people aren't fond of James, because he talks a lot about works. But I love that the apostle James brings balance and accountability to the believer—and to me, because I need it! While I know God loves me no matter what I do, I also need to know that disobedience does interfere with my progress and growth. I'm certainly no theologian, but I've been on the holy highway for a mighty long spell, and I've noted that I'm often my biggest obstacle to overcome along the way.

Come join me. Let's crack open the book and see what James has to say about hardships: "Consider it a sheer gift, friends, when tests and challenges come at you from all sides. You know that under pressure, your faith-life is forced into the open and shows its true colors. So don't try to get out of anything prematurely. Let it do its work so you become mature and well-developed, not deficient in any way" (James 1:2–4 MSG).

Hardship is a gift? Well, I don't want it under my Christmas tree! It's just natural to bolt and run when life tightens up. I guess that's why James had to tell us to sit tight and be thankful. Note that he didn't say sit and sulk. I've survived pressing circumstances—some I've learned from; others I've only endured. (I sat, but I wasn't exactly thankful, mature, or well developed—which was my loss.)

Even though this is a tall order from James, it's also full of hope. When I understand that pain, loss, and difficulty have a purpose, a work to do within me, I can learn to see meaning in my suffering. The Lord gives me "honey from the rock"

(Psalm 81:16), and I'm grateful James reminds me of it. I don't know how God does it; I'm just grateful he does.

That's why I love to read; it broadens my perspective. It takes me off the page I'm living on and opens up new angles of insight. Reading expands my vocabulary, improves my conversational skills, and nudges me away from ingrown opinions.

When we add Scripture to our reading menu, we have the delicious benefit of God's sweet counsel, even when it's startling and goes against our nature. Unsettling as it can be, God's Word prepares me to face scallywags and helps me to survive deeply thrust daggers.

I didn't become a reader all at once; it was more a page-by-page process. So go ahead, turn the page, and answer the Cracked-Up Questions.

*Lord, thank you for being the author and the finisher of my story. May you cause the pages of my existence to be fresh with spiritual vigor. Help me to passionately follow you until the last word of my story is written. Amen.*

## Cracked-Up Questions

**If your life were a book, what would you title it?**

**Think about a time when your life felt like fiction.**

**What scallywags are on your horizon?**

**How has hardship served your character?**

**List your current reading menu.**

## Just for FuN

### Cracker Jack

Cracker Jack, that wonderful confection of popcorn, peanuts, and molasses, was introduced to the world—literally—at the first World's Fair in Chicago, 1893. People loved the treat but found it too sticky. So inventor Louis Rueckheim and his brother, Frederick, developed a formula that made the molasses coating crispy but dry. To this day, that formula is still used and remains a secret.

In 1896, a salesperson sampled the popcorn morsel and exclaimed, "That's a crackerjack!"—which meant it was exceptionally good. The brothers snatched up the name and trademarked it.

Initially, Cracker Jack was sold in large tubs, but in 1899, the company decided to package the snack in a special wax-covered box that kept the candy fresh longer. The popular snack grew in fame when, in 1908, it was mentioned in the song "Take Me Out to the Ball Game": "Take me out to the ball game; take me out to the crowd. Buy me some peanuts and Cracker Jack . . ."

And then came the prizes. In 1910, the company offered coupons in the boxes, which children could send in to receive prizes. But the process was cumbersome, so someone came up with the idea of just tucking the prizes in the box. Avid collectors have their own Cracker Jack conventions. Among some of the most sought-after items are animal prizes, each of which stood for a letter of the alphabet. Collectors work to acquire sets all in the same color.

Speaking of color, the box developed its red, white, and blue patriotic design during World War I. Sailor Jack was added about 1916, along with his dog, Bingo. They were modeled after Frederick's grandson and his dog.

All in all, Cracker Jack was a crackerjack idea!

# 10

# Like a Diamond in the Sky

I've been studying about hope . . . the Hope Diamond, that is. Did you know that the Hope Diamond started off at more than 112 carats, but today it's just over 45 carats? Talk about broken. Wouldn't you love to have a chip off that block?

Now, when I say only 45 carats, that's compared to its original size, which is, shall we say, outside of my grocery budget. Why, I have a friend with a five-carat diamond ring, and she needs help just to tote her hand around. I've offered to literally take it off her hands, but so far, no deal. And I thought it such a friendly gesture!

Imagine a diamond as large as your fist, which was the size of the Hope when it was first purchased by a French merchant. It must have been an astounding sight. He said it was a beautiful violet color. Later, the diamond would be known as a French blue, and today it is a dark grayish-blue. Hmm, if it keeps this up, maybe it will go on sale, and I could (cough, cough) pick it up for a song and a dance.

The Hope Diamond is believed to have originated in the

Kollur mine in India, but it has now traveled throughout the world and has had many owners. It was even stolen in 1772 and disappeared for years before resurfacing in 1812, in a collection owned by a London diamond merchant.

Hope (I hope she doesn't mind if I call her by her first name) spent years in the possession of French royalty. In 1673, the stone was cut down to 67 carats, set in gold, and suspended on a neck ribbon for King Louis XIV to wear on ceremonial occasions. I'm surprised the king didn't need neck traction after carting that boulder around, although had I been he, I might have risked it as well.

Actually, what the diamond, throughout its career, has mostly been used for is paying off debts. Just imagine—hocking your Hope.

In 1910, Mrs. Evalyn Walsh McLean of Washington, D.C., saw the Hope Diamond at Cartier's in Paris, but (get this) she didn't like the setting. Cartier had it reset on a headpiece on a three-tiered circlet of large white diamonds, which appealed to Mrs. McLean, so she purchased it. Later, she had a neck chain of white diamonds designed to hold the Hope gem, which was set into a sixteen-diamond pendant. Soldered onto the pendant was a bail so that other diamonds might be hung from it.

Good golly, Mrs. McLean, was that not a tad redundant? But then I've heard it said that "diamonds are a girl's best friend." And I suppose you can't have too many friends.

After Mrs. McLean's death, her entire jewelry collection was sold to Harry Winston, Inc., of New York. Later, on November 10, 1958, they would donate . . . yes, *donate*, the

Hope necklace to the Smithsonian. Not surprisingly, the diamond immediately became the Smithsonian's premier attraction.

There's just something about bling that's captivating . . . much like true hope. Hope, that glorious light at the end of the tunnel, is a multifaceted, brilliant dimension of life. If you've ever experienced hope or observed it in another person, you know that it's indescribable yet undeniable. It's appealing and priceless.

Yet even with all the influence and financial resources of the Smithsonian, that museum can't purchase or display hope in a tangible form. It's not for sale at a jewelry store. And sometimes we can't demand a new setting.

But hope often is unearthed in the dark mines of hospital wards, funeral parlors, senior homes, rehab centers, prison cells, abuse centers, counselors' offices, etc. It's the "etc." I especially appreciate, because that includes every arena of life. Hope is an equal-opportunity employer.

Hope can seem elusive and outside of our price range when, in fact, it's available to pauper and prince alike, thanks to Jesus.

I sometimes wish I could wear my hope as a pendant so all who see it might be drawn to my dazzling Christ. But isn't that what happens when we live out our faith in spite of hardships and opposition? What looks impossible suddenly glistens with hope, and others come to observe and ask questions.

Ever notice how a dark velvet backdrop enhances a diamond's qualities? So, too, does hope shine on a backdrop of pain, failure, and loss. Like Corrie ten Boom's life, which included a death camp, or Mother Teresa's, which included the poverty and sicknesses of India. Their diamond-studded lives continue to glitter and refract Christ's hope. There's the Old Testament Joseph, who spent years forgotten in a dank prison yet came forth as royalty. Or Daniel, sitting in the dark mine of false accusations and the immediate threat of wild animals. Yet he came forth like a radiant gem. And Shadrach, Meshach, and Abed-Nego, who went through the fiery furnace and came forth unharmed.

What unlikely candidates they must have appeared with their situations seemingly beyond hope. Yet that's what hope is—the unlikely, even the impossible, becoming the absolute.

*Lord, hope keeps us when life cheats us, because we know you can redeem the unredeemable. You can take the unholy and transform it into the holy. When everyone else has given up, you continue steadfast, working out all things. How grateful we are for your provision of the stunning gem of hope. May we wear it well and become a premier attraction for you. Amen.*

## Cracked-Up Questions

**What erodes hope?**

**Who or what has chipped away at your hope?**

**Does hope change shape, size, or color?**
**If so, how and why?**

**How does Christ dazzle you?**

**Is anything beyond God's control or ability to perform?**
**If so, what?**

# 11

# My Kind of Catering

On an ordinary day, an unsuspecting mom rises early to see her children off for school. Like hundreds of other days, she packs their lunches, making sure they have enough food to keep them healthy and strong. Then she shoos them along and sets off to run her errands.

Her son—let's call him Jim—is on his way to class, and he passes streams of people headed to the mountain near the seaside. Their chatter catches his ear, and the next thing he knows, he has joined the crowd. After arriving at their destination, he finds a small rock and sits down on it to see what will happen next.

A man stood, and when he did, Jim's heart fluttered with wonder at the man's countenance. So humble, so holy . . . like a priest, only more.

The crowds hushed.

Words were exchanged between the man and his disciples, and Jim wondered what they spoke about. Then the disciples turned and walked toward the young boy. Jim's heart was thumping hard as one of the disciples approached him. Kneeling next to Jim, the disciple asked if the boy would be willing to give his lunch to Jesus.

Jim didn't hesitate but extended his fish and barley loaves, thinking the man they called Jesus was hungry. Even though the boy didn't know Jesus, Jim was so drawn to the man that Jim wanted to give Jesus all he had.

When the fish and bread were presented to Jesus, he prayed over them, giving thanks. Then he handed the boy's lunch to his disciples, who then distributed it to the crowd of thousands.

Five barley loaves and two small fish—to feed five thousand people. Why, that's hardly an appetizer for me—and they had leftovers!

I've wondered what happened when the little boy ran home and told his mom about his lunch-capade. Do you think she gave him time-out for telling a whopper? Or applauded him for his creativity? Or thought he was just giving another excuse to get out of eating his fish? Or perhaps word had already reached his mom that her faithfulness in taking care of her family had blessed multitudes.

Sometimes I wonder if anyone notices the little things I do to make a meal more appealing, a card more personal, or a house cozier. I know we shouldn't wait for applause, but truth be known, sometimes I do. Don't you? I don't need much—just a nod, smile, or affirming comment. "How pretty!" works. Or, "Isn't that clever?"

I doubt Jim's mom received a lot of accolades about her sack lunches. Yet she faithfully prepared the meal for her children each day. Then one of her lunches reached thousands. What made the difference? Jesus blessed it. And that's when the miracle occurred.

I think everything unpacks more fully when we ask Jesus to bless what we have. The little we possess becomes much when holy breath consecrates it. And you'll note the lunch became humongous when the boy chose to share it. He could have decided he wouldn't hand over his midday meal, that he was hungry enough to wolf it down while the crowd watched him. That tells me that in sharing comes a special blessing. Not sharing out of my abundance but out of my meager bit.

Think of it . . . Jesus could have had store-bought groceries available for his drop-in guests, but instead he chose to use a child's lunch. That must have been the most important day of that boy's life.

And what a lesson it is for us! Bring whatever you have to offer, and let God bless it. You have no idea how he'll unpack it. However he does, you do know it will add to your sense of significance, and it will honor him.

*Lord, you do so much with our modest offerings. We don't deserve your extravagance, but we thank you for it. Deliver us from the addiction of applause. May it be enough that we delight you. Now take the barley loaves and fish of our lives, and bless them. Amen.*

## Cracked-Up Questions

**What's in your lunch bag? Are you ready to hand it over to Jesus?**

**Do you believe in miracles? If so, why? If not, why not?**

**Tell about a time you witnessed a miracle or a time your heart fluttered with wonder over something God did.**

**Do you have Jesus-generosity? What one thing could you do to move more in that direction?**

# 12

# Animal Quackers, Anyone?

*Animal crackers and cocoa to drink,*
*That is the finest of suppers I think.*
—Christopher Morely

I've been known to share Christopher Morely's enthusiasm for animal crackers and cocoa, partaking of that late-night snack, which is sure to induce sleep and add tonnage.

When I grew up, one of the funner treats was to receive a box of animal crackers. I recall studying each shape and loudly proclaiming that animal's name. Sometimes I would skip down the sidewalk, swinging the circus-motif box on its string handle. Talk about a great combo—it was a purse filled with food!

Shirley Temple suggested another way to consume the cookies in the film *Curly Top* when she sang, "Animal crackers in my soup, monkeys and rabbits loop the loop." Lions and tigers and bears, oh my!

These "quacker" tidbits existed in England as early as the late 1800s as mammal-shaped, fancy cookies. By the end of the nineteenth century, American bakeries were producing the cookies and calling them "animals" or "circus crackers." Then the bakeries united and began to distribute the goodies nationally.

Packaging was key to their success. Named "animal biscuits" or "Barnum's animals," at Christmastime the cookies were contained in a box designed to look like a circus wagon with a string attached so it could be hung as a tree ornament. The boxes sold for five cents and were an immediate hit.

And the crackers were quite a menagerie. Since 1902, thirty-seven different animals have been featured on crackers in those little stringed boxes. Seventeen varieties are currently available: tigers, cougars, camels, rhinoceroses, kangaroos, hippopotami, bison, lions, hyenas, zebras, elephants, sheep, bears, gorillas, monkeys, seals, and giraffes. Can you spell *zoo*?

Speaking of zoos, I'm sure Noah felt as if he were in a little box on a string, with a bunch of critters going bananas all around him. Talk about having a tiger by the tail!

I find it interesting that Noah's name, according to my Bible dictionary, means "to rest." Ha! That's one of the experiences Noah probably didn't have on the ark. Imagine feeding all those beasties and keeping the place . . . cleaned up, shall we say? He must have owned one enormous pooper-scooper!

But my Bible dictionary postulates that Noah's name might also mean "God brings relief." Now, that makes more sense.

First of all, Noah had neighbors who would make anyone

feel cracked up. Their dissipated lifestyles were something to behold, I'm sure. Then Noah had to put up with several years of razzing as he built a seeming monument to insanity. "A boondoggle for sure," the neighbors proclaimed. "If we had any water—which we don't!—bet that thing wouldn't even float." Not to mention their complaints that it was cluttering up the landscape, a real eyesore devaluing their homes.

I can just hear Noah mutter, "Give me a break, Lord," about the time those first drops of water plunked against the boat. Just the sound brought blessed relief. Then again, there was the corralling of the animals, feeding them, and cleaning up their mess. Probably, just about the time Noah was moaning, "I can't take it anymore, Lord," the skies cleared. Ah, sweet relief.

But then everyone onboard had to wait for the flooded terrain to simmer down. By that time, all the family members were on one another's last nerve, don't you think?

Finally, the dove returned with the olive branch of peace. Ah, God-sponsored relief. But even sweeter to Noah than the knowledge that he could disembark and let loose the animals was the display of God's enduring promise of rest that he saw: a rainbow.

Doesn't seeing a rainbow flood you with rest, awe, and amazement? While some people understand the scientific reason behind rainbows, I've always found those explanations real yawners. I like to think of rainbows as a signal that God is present and cares. They're symbols of rest for the weary, broken, and disheartened.

A few months ago, as I was driving home from the airport after a tiring trip, I glanced out the window and saw a double rainbow. It was vividly colored, almost neon, and so close. For a minute I thought about rushing over for those pots of gold. But then I remembered that rainbows *are* pots of gold, shining with God's love. And that's priceless—even better than animal crackers and hot cocoa.

> *Lord, I thank you for your multihued loving-kindness, which you choose to express in our lives each day. I appreciate that you know we need visual reminders of your constancy, and that you picked the rainbow as one of those memory enhancers. Refresh my recollection of your love, peace, and rest. Help me to remember that, in you, I can nestle in and find sweet relief from today's pressures.*

## Cracked-Up Questions

**What was your favorite childhood snack?**

**Can you remember a specific time you spotted a rainbow and were reminded of God's presence?**

**Where do you turn for rest when your soul is weary?**

**What visual reminders might you use to help you to remember that relief is found in God?**

# 13

# Fit for a King

Back in the days of butlers and maids, a woman's chinaware was selected carefully to display her good taste and expansive budget. Should a china plate chip or crack, it was tossed onto the rubbish heap. And heaven forbid a hostess even think about using an odd-man-out plate rather than replace the whole kit and caboodle. Why, you'd think every woman of means was preparing to serve a king!

The following paragraph, published in 1931 on behalf of a large department store, introduced the virtues of open-stock china and glassware, which apparently was a relatively new concept. Picture the article writer with a snooty look on his smug face as he extols the importance of proper choices in one's hundred-piece set of china:

> *China and Glassware.* Here are two ancient and closely allied products from which the shopper expects paradoxical virtues. Primarily associated with the dining room, they are expected both to give the appearance of fragility on the

> table and to demonstrate their ruggedness in the butler's pantry. Should a plate or glass be dropped in the dining room, the shopper, as hostess, would be mortified to see it bounce undamaged on the floor; but, as housewife, she wants that same plate or glass to withstand chipping or cracking in the sink.

Well, pardon me. I guess my dishwasher-safe and chip-resistant dinnerware wouldn't pass muster. Nor would my collection of odds-and-ends glasses. And certainly not my mix-and-match table settings.

Yet in this starched world of yesteryear, one type of cracked dish was held in high regard. Called "crackleware," these pottery items were designed with delicate, weblike cracks. They were greatly prized because crafting crackleware was a lost art for two hundred years. Developed in the Ming Dynasty in 1644, crackleware was initially known as "Dragon's Blood" because the cracked veins were a vibrant red. A Massachusetts potter, Hugh Cornwall Robertson, saw the ancient pottery at the 1876 Philadelphia Centennial Exhibition. Fascinated by the beauty of the vases, he set out to rediscover the process.

Ten years later (talk about dedication!) he succeeded, but it wasn't until 1904—almost twenty years after figuring out the process—that Robertson's work was truly recognized. That year, he sent his choicest pieces to the St. Louis World's Exposition, where the judges declared his vases equal to the priceless Ming pottery. Four years later, Robertson died after being awarded prizes throughout the world for his beautifully crafted crackleware.

Robertson's perseverance, working quietly in the background, is a quality I don't relate to. "Perseverance" and "Patsy" are seldom used in the same sentence. But his product—a cracked pot? Now that's a good fit for me.

It's not as if the Bible doesn't provide me with good examples of folks who patiently persevered, working in the background until they were called center stage to strut their stuff. Why, Moses was so far offstage, it took a burning bush to get him to move in the right direction. But while he waited in the desert, he learned his way around the wilderness—a skill that would come in handy for forty years and millions of people.

Joseph was thrown in prison, where he spent years learning the Egyptian language. He could have despaired, but instead he used that time to prepare for God's call.

David was out in the field watching the sheep and learning how to take on lions, tigers, and bears when Samuel came calling to anoint David king.

Gideon was threshing wheat on his farm when an angel popped in for a little visit and an assignment to lead the Israelite army. Gideon used household items—jars and trumpets—to defeat the enemy. (Now, that's what I call a good use of cracked pottery.)

James and John were fishing for fish when Jesus called them to fish for men. As a side note, fishing is considered a quiet sport, but I suspect these two brothers were going about their work with a lot of shouting and horsing around. After all, they were called the Sons of Thunder—could that mean they were impetuous and undisciplined? We're talking my language here!

Moses, David, Gideon, James, and John all remind us that we should go about the business God has appointed for us today—whether that's tossing out our chipped china saucers, puzzling over a long-lost process (like remembering how to cook), or tending the garden.

The Lord is perfectly capable of finding me wherever I am and calling me forward for his service. Or just leaving me to my weeds. It's his choice; mine is to persevere—preferably quietly—and to make sure I'm fit to serve the King.

*Lord, help me to remember you have wonderfully made me just as I am. Help me also to remember that I can gain from working on my weaknesses and that perseverance pays off, sometimes in unexpected ways, sometimes in invisible ways. Help me to know how I can prepare myself to be fit for your service.*

## Cracked-Up Questions

**Recall a time you displayed more perseverance than you thought you had.**

**Would you describe yourself as someone who can work quietly in the background or as someone who yearns to be center stage?**

**Where has God placed you now?**

**What do you think he wants you to learn during this time?**

# 14

# You Gotta Have Heart

As an agoraphobic who couldn't leave my house, I was scrunched between the bookends of fear and anger, living a constricted life. My emotional blinders made it difficult to see beyond my own consuming needs. So when my gradual healing began, the door to the world cracked open ever so slowly, allowing me, little by little, to see more of its beauties. One of those beauties was art.

Growing up, art conjured up for me pictures of baked enamel pins, teachers in smocks, and clay creations of squatty thumbprint animals—though mine always looked pretty much like thumbprints. I don't remember hearing about Monet, Manet, or even Michelangelo. Not that I was listening. But when my art appetite was finally whetted as an adult, I developed a fervent interest. Today, I love to visit art museums, peruse books of great art, and have lively discussions about art.

Luci Swindoll is a work of art. She has, with generous brushstrokes, invested in me and countless others, encouraging us to experience paintings, statues, cathedrals, and architecture. From her, I have learned of egg and dart, of Seurat, Pollock, and Degas. Luci's enthusiasm is contagious, and her appreciation for fine art has been highly polished by her family, her bachelor's degree in that field, and her worldwide travels that have allowed her to visit museums around the globe.

Luci also gave me one of my favorite books—a beautiful edition of Sister Wendy's *1000 Masterpieces*. Sister Wendy's commentary on the masterpieces is witty and enlightening. Even a novice like me gets to see with painterly eyes. She walks you inside the paintings and directs your attention to the details that add depth and meaning.

Now, I confess that some of the paintings crack me up. I don't understand a few of the Sister's choices. I don't care how much information I read; I think they are a bit odd, even bizarre. But then, my art training for years was limited to Crayolas, an Etch A Sketch, and a box of Lite Brites. My way of perusing an art gallery was to thumb through the latest Beetle Bailey and Baby Huey comic books. And my idea of a grand "statue" was one we passed once a year on vacation when I was a kid—a fifteen-foot-tall neon sign the shape of a farmer's daughter toting her straw hat outside a restaurant in Illinois.

Today, my favorite statue is one I've only seen in pictures, starting at Luci's house in a framed poster above her fireplace. It has several names and stands in the Louvre in Paris. In fact, it's touted as one of the museum's greatest treasures. A marble sculpture of a Greek goddess, it was discovered in 1863. It's best known to us as Winged Victory or Nike.

What draws me to this figure is her name, Victory, and her elegant grace in spite of significant damage. The sculpture has lost her head—literally. (If only I were as graceful when I lose my head!) Draped in marble, the folds of her garments fall like rare silk. Her outstretched wings appear luminous and ready for flight. Victory originally was designed for the bow of a ship, proclaiming its triumphant fleet. She is believed to have had outstretched arms with an extended trumpet that she used to blow a victory song. In 1950, one of Victory's hands was found and is now displayed in a glass case next to the statue.

Victory is just over ten feet of marble splendor. Her broken beauty is simultaneously strong and fragile. Her remains are a picture of defiance against the odds and of beauty, not only in spite of hardship, but also because of it. Many feel the statue's brokenness enhances its depiction of the supernatural.

I think the aspect I love most about art is its ability to inspire. When I'm functioning "headless," Victory reminds me that my heart can carry me through. When I'm feeling helpless to assist others, as if my hands were encased, I'm reminded that I can rely on God's supernatural work. It's OK if I'm damaged by life's adversities; I can still stand strong because the Lord makes his strength known in our weakness.

Hmm, all those insights from a statue . . . Imagine if she could talk. Oh, I guess she has—and without saying a word.

*Lord, it's amazing to think that a marble slab can have heart, but then should that surprise us when you offer to transform our hearts from stone to flesh? When we feel helpless, you do for us what we can't do for ourselves. Thank you that you breathed into us the breath of life and offer us the ability to set a solid example for others, even to inspire them. Yes, you are truly impressive, Lord. Amen.*

## Cracked-Up Questions

**How were you exposed to art as a child? (Yes, comic books count!)**

**What can you do to learn more about appreciating art?**

**What is your favorite work of art?**

**Why is art important?**

**Are you feeling victorious in your life? Why?**

**Can you think of anyone whose brokenness has added to her beauty?**

## Just for FuN

# Cracked-Up Locales

Get out your map and prepare yourself for a fun-filled journey.

Have you ever been to Monkey Eyebrow, Kentucky, or Bald Head, Maine? Me neither. Don't you wonder how they got their handles? What about Unalaska, Alaska? That made me titter. Do you think they were so remote they weren't sure they still belonged?

And get this—there is a Nowhere, Oklahoma, and a No Name, Colorado. Can you hear it now: "And where do you live?"

"Nowhere."

"You have to live somewhere."

"I do."

"Where?"

"Nowhere."

Hmm, maybe they ought to move to Why Not, North Carolina. No, I didn't make that up. Then there's always Ubet, Wisconsin; Useful, Missouri; or Uno, Kentucky.

Of course, if you're hankering for something tasty, you might want to try Bread Loaf, Vermont; Chicken, Alaska; or Buttermilk, Kansas.

Want to avoid junk mail? Then move to Yreka Zzyzx, California, or Quonochontaug, Rhode Island. I can't pronounce them, and I bet mailers can't spell them.

If you seem to be running a streak of bad luck, you might consider Sucker Flat, California; Tickfaw, Louisana; Idiotville, Oregon; or Zap, North Dakota.

For those days when we want to squawk, Yellville, Arkansas, might hold appeal or maybe Fickle, Indiana, for those times when we are full of ourselves.

But my all-time favorites are Hallelujah Junction, California, and Little Heaven, Delaware. How fun to invite folks to visit our little corner of Heaven or to write Hallelujah on every envelope.

And if you want to seal every letter with a kiss, think about U-Hauling over to Sweet Lips, Tennessee.

Lest you think our nation forgot an all-cracked-up approach when naming locations, check out this list:

Broken Arrow, Oklahoma (known as B.A. to locals)

Brokenstraw Township, Pennsylvania (so named because the annual crop at one time was tall prairie grass that would break and fall over in the autumn)

Breakneck Pond, Connecticut (which is truly a pond—one I'd rather not swim in)

Cracker Jack, Pennsylvania (the word *crackerjack* means "excellent" or "superb")

Crack in the Ground, Oregon (not far from Hole in the Ground—honest!)

Crackers Neck, Virginia (ouch!)

Stonebreaker Crossing, California

Y'all come, hear!

# 15

# Swallow Hard

Let me say right up front to all the birders reading this book, I love soaring, singing, nesting creatures. I've faithfully watched birds for years. I'm an Audubon fan, I read John Muir's works, and I have twenty pounds of birdseed stockpiled in my garage. I even keep a bird journal.

But for weeks on end, swallows have been trying to build a nest over my entry door. I am a hospitable woman; I enjoy visitors, and I even have myriad feeders for the feathered ones. But this multitasking swallow couple keeps slathering mud and twigs onto our brick while dropping sizable white donations on our welcome mat. How rude is that? From a distance, it looks like mounds of snow are covering our doorstep, but it's July. And if it were snow, I could shovel it. But this contrary stuff has to be chiseled away.

We have tried to shoo off the birds in a friendly manner. "Shoo, shoo!" I've called out, arms flailing in the breeze like a windmill. But do they listen? No. Instead they swoop down at my head, as if *I'm* the intruder.

"Go find a tree!" I've shouted to them more than once. They're welcome to any branch, bush, or begonia in our yard, but the threshold of my home is out of bounds.

As the swallow couple has continued to paste their mud wads on our house, they have left us no alternative but to knock down their adobe ledge, lest they baptize our arriving guests in nesting materials and other stuff. (It's the other stuff I'm most worried about. Have you ever been hit? Not nice. And when it dries? Ugh.)

Yet, no matter how many times we have toppled their domain, the swallows have returned. It hasn't even ruffled their feathers when they have found yet another nest swept away. Day in and day out, they keep starting over. I must admit, I almost admire their tenacity; I mean, obviously, the mama swallow taught them well. I think she skipped over the lessons on Know Where You're Not Wanted, Moving On, Potty Etiquette, and Nest Nice, but at least they're outside.

I've always felt bad for birds that have inadvertently flown into a mall and can't get out. But now I'm considering transporting these two mudslingers to the nearest shopping center for, let's say, a spree. Don't worry, I'd give them gift certificates before abandoning them; and when I shopped there, I'd even drop bread crumbs.

A friend suggested before "malling" them that I should try talking to the birds and let them know of my displeasure. I realize that sounds ludicrous, but, hey, I was desperate. So as they sat side by side on my eaves waiting for their next chance to invade my porch, I stepped out and explained how unacceptable their housing plan was.

I told them that every neighborhood had building codes and that ours didn't allow multiple families living on the same property. During my negotiations, I even sang a short chorus of "When the Swallows Fly Back to Capistrano" and offered them a detailed, highlighted map. They chirped in response, which heartened me.

But once I walked back inside my house, Mr. and Mrs. Birdbrain proceeded with what appeared to be renewed vigor to fling mud and drop potty-bombs in the confines of my entry. So much for the Dr. Doolittle approach.

I know you're waiting for me to tell you how we finally rid ourselves of these nesting nuisances, but alas, the battle wages on. It's part of our routine: knock down nest, use hose on porch splats, chisel and sweep chunky debris into garden, say unpleasant things as featherheads swoop down.

I wonder if the For Sale sign in front of our house drew the swallows to begin with. Who knows? Maybe they want to buy the place. They've sure left big enough deposits.

*Lord, we are battling an ever-present intruder in our lives. He is persistent, devious, unteachable, and destructive. His goal is to distract us from what's important and to cause us to use up our strength. Nothing would please him more than to wreck our home, steal our peace, and leave us in the stench of his continual efforts. Thank you that, even though the battle continues, you have his address as well as ours. May we beware of his swooping antics but not befuddled by them. Thank you that you have defeated him, and we are safe as we nest near your heart. Amen.*

## Cracked-Up Questions

Who disrupts your home life?

What have you done to change that?
Has it been effective?

In what areas of your life are you tenacious?

What part of your life might you need
to start over . . . again?

Whose feathers have you recently ruffled?
Who has ruffled yours?

Do you "nest nice"? List three ways to do that.

16

# Cloudy Weather

*The sky is low, the clouds are mean,*
*A travelling flake of snow*
*Across a barn or through a rut*
*Debates if it will go.*

*A narrow wind complains all day*
*How some one treated him;*
*Nature, like us, is sometimes caught*
*Without her diadem.*

—Emily Dickinson

Today, for as far as I can see, there's not a cloud in the sky, not even a wisp. But I know from experience that Texas really knows how to put on a storm.

Les and I were there this past winter, and they swirled up a dandy for us. Big clouds, like billowing hot air balloons, chased each other across the afternoon sky. At first, they were fluffy and friendly; but soon they turned menacing and mean. Even their color changed dramatically from new-linen white to scruffy gray until finally they were raging ebony. Cloud murmurs soon became freight-train roars and were pierced through by silver daggers of lightning. And then, much to our fascination and chagrin, hail ricocheted off the roof and windows. First, pinging sounds erupted everywhere, like a popcorn machine gone ballistic, and then the sounds intensified as the hail swelled to fat marbles and Ping-Pong balls. It got a little exciting!

After a thunderous pounding, the hail subsided and the clouds scurried out as quickly as they had galloped in. We were left with mounds of hail covering our patio furniture; amazed, we scooped it off by the handfuls. As we did, I couldn't help thinking back to those Israelites and their manna. Not only did they have holy crackers covering their yards, but they also had a cloud guiding them for forty years on their way to the Promised Land. Now *that's* amazing.

The cloud was to keep God's people from trailing off in the wrong direction; it was a reminder of God's constant presence and his promise that he would lead them to a better land. At night, the cloud turned into a pillar of fire. I can imagine it casting light like a giant, flaming torch that must have brought the people, even those camping on the back forty, a sense of safety. It was a divine nightlight.

Most importantly, the cloud was the vehicle God chose to speak through. I wonder what his voice sounded like. Thunder? Wind? Hail? I do know that the people weren't eager to hear his voice directly, because they knew it was an awesome and fearful thing to be in God's presence. So they left that to Moses and the priests. The people's job was to keep their eyes on the cloud and to follow it.

Isn't that our job as well? Not cloud watching or storm chasing or weather forecasting, but keeping our focus heavenward. In the book of Colossians, we're instructed to "set [our minds] on things above" (3:2), to "seek those things which are above" (3:1), and to remember that our hope is in heaven (1:5). And I believe it's because not all clouds on earth are friendly.

Actually, we just had a not-so-friendly heap of clouds and wind in Michigan; the super-cell type of storm that can create tornados hit our little town. It swirled about, causing havoc and leaving in its wake splintered memories. Its huffing and puffing lasted only a few moments, but when those clouds finally took a breath and fled, one-hundred-year-old maples and giant oaks lay across rooftops and roads. I saw with my own eyes that Texas isn't the only place that knows how to throw a storm.

From sea to shining sea, tempests are to be expected in our weather patterns and in our lives. Try as you might, you can't find a picture-perfect weather spot in the world.

But do we want to? No clouds and no rain equals no green terrain. Why, our gardens would be stubble, our trees stumps, flowers dried-up seeds, and our wells dust. Makes one want to sing, "Let it rain, let it rain, let it rain."

Clouds are typecast according to how far off the ground they are—high level, midlevel, and low level. Depending on their height, they are composed of water droplets, ice crystals, ice particles, or snow. The moisture content in the clouds, when touched by the light of the evening sun, creates the magnificent array of colors in a sunset.

That's true of our lives as well. Clouds will blow through our neighborhoods, whether we live in Texas or Michigan. Some will be fair-weather friends, while others will pummel us with the hail of hardships and swirls of sorrow. While we may have to step through the cleanup, we know the Son will once again fill our skies with color.

*Lord, whatever the weather, you have promised to be with us. Your covenant fills our darkest skies with rainbow potential. Remind us that the rain, and even the storms, provide the life-giving moisture necessary to keep us spiritually lush. You are God not only of the sun but also of the clouds, which causes us to crown them with importance. Keep our eyes ever on you. Amen.*

## Cracked-Up Questions

**How's the weather in your life?**

**What clouds are on your horizon?**

**What's the worst storm you've been in (physically, relationally, emotionally)?**

## Just for Fun

### Cracked-Up Sounds

The crackle of bacon

The crack of ice you're standing on (Run!)

The crack of a boy's voice when it's changing

A crack of thunder

Cracking open a book

Firecracker

The crack of dawn (You must rise up early, lean in, and listen hard.)

The crackle of aging knees (Ask me!)

Cracking crab

The crack of a cannon

A wisecrack

Cracking an egg

The crackle of breakfast cereal

The crack of a breaking branch

The crack of a whip

Cracking one's knuckles

Cracking up with laughter

# Part 2

# Wisecrackers

*We can learn much from wise words, little from wisecracks, and less from wise guys.*

—William Arthur Ward

# 17

# Baby, It's Cold Inside!

I just came in from doing three jumping jacks, four knee bends, and jogging around the mailbox twice. Nope, I'm not on a new exercise program; I just needed to warm up. Not for a marathon, I assure you.

See, Les has a habit of cranking our house thermostat down to the chill factor of Antarctica, so I periodically have to deice my bones. I've become accustomed to the frost dangling off my eyebrows, but the icicles in my sandals still annoy me. I think it's those pointy ends. Here's the bottom line: when one must wear flannel pj's and thick socks to bed in July (hello, July!), something's amiss with wedded bliss.

Les and I just celebrated forty-three years of marriage, so I know I should be used to how differently we are calibrated. But when I have to leave the house just to thaw out, it rankles me a tad. In addition to maintaining a year-round winter freeze, Les has a need to crunch ice, a glassful at a time. Of course, I have a need to gripe about his crunching ice, a glassful at a time. Isn't it great how we meet each other's needs?

Living with a person isn't easy. Living alone isn't easy. Actually, living isn't easy. Worthwhile, certainly, but not easy. Why, even breathing can be tedious, especially if each breath turns to frozen crystals and then shatters at one's feet.

Ice-crunching Les loves Willie Nelson at high decibels, while I like the warmth of Bucelli played whisper-soft. Les likes a slab of cow on a tin plate, and I like gourmet goodies on a sterling tray. Les loves two big, fat pillows to sleep on, while I sleep pillowless. (You already knew I was strange—I make no apologies.) Les likes spaghetti westerns, while I'm into spaghetti pie and *Breakfast at Tiffany's*. Les drives a honkin' SUV, and I drive a wee PT Cruiser. Les wants to safari in Africa, while I want to invite friends into our home for tea. Can you feel the tension?

We both have seasonal spells where we want to cook . . . just not together. It comes on us suddenly, often at the same time, like an outbreak of measles. It never lasts long for either of us, but we've found it best not to be in the proximity of kitchen utensils at the same time. We're quite territorial. In fact, it's better if we take different shifts in the kitchen. That way, nobody gets skewered (unintentionally, of course).

It didn't happen all at once, but along our marriage path, Les and I have learned to celebrate each other's differences. Oh, all right, "celebrate" might be a bit Pollyanna-ish, but we have learned to make space and extend grace. Marriage is, in part, learning to tolerate each other's peculiarities and, when possible, to applaud them. That would be where the grace comes in.

Les and I confess we are quite competitive. We both like to be right; we have a rightness addiction. And more often than we should, we both think we are. Although, I must say, it's easier to acquiesce to each other today than when we were married teenagers. In those chaotic years, we were in constant power struggles, mood swings, and identity tussles.

Today, we are in a much sweeter place because of Christ's intervening love, which has breached the gap between our human efforts. Also, years can bring (no guarantee) much needed maturity. Yet, if I'm honest, we're still capable of being at odds over the silliest things, which reminds us of our frailty and our ongoing need for a Savior.

I must say that while Les makes me shiver with the temperature in our home, he melts me with the warmth of his thoughtfulness. He's kind, funny, and generous. He's also romantic, supportive, and protective. So between you and me, what are a few extra layers of fleece-lined clothes, sporadic outdoor aerobics, and a hefty bagful of earplugs?

Crunch away, big boy; you're my kind of guy!

*Lord, how quickly we deplete our love supply for one another. Even our best efforts can be tainted by manipulation. Help us to reach past ourselves, and deliver us from the addiction of proclaiming, "I was right!" Instead, may we respond with a servant's heart, as you did on our behalf. When we feel put out with someone else, remind us of how you put up with us. Give us eyes of mercy as we look upon those around us, and grow our hearts to fit your love. Amen.*

## Cracked-Up Questions

What's the coldest you've ever been?

What habits of others get on your last nerve?

Which is easier: changing others or changing yourself?

What would you have to do to change?

How does being right differ from doing right?

How should knowing we are made in God's image affect our behavior toward each other?

# 18

# Art Thou Cracked?

Imagine taking a gigantic piece of stone, say fourteen feet tall, and chiseling a figure out of it. (Actually, I can't even imagine having the courage to climb a scaffold that high, let alone seeing what to do with that hunk of rock!) Now imagine carving not just any figure but one of the most famous images in art, the statue of David. That's what Michelangelo did.

That sounds pretty amazing, wouldn't you say? But even more astounding is that the piece of granite Michelangelo used was riddled with cracks. Not only was the marble full of fissures, but some other sculptor had already tried to use the massive rock, creating a crack that caused a chunk of marble to fall off. Why, that rock had so many cracks that no other artist considered working with it. Talk about a reject!

What did Michelangelo see in that slab of stone that no one else did? After three years of intense labor, the finished work was unveiled. Today art aficionados can see that Michelangelo worked around his material's limitations, shifting David's weight onto his right leg to counter the big crack. Seeing the piece's flaws, he managed to make it into something magnificent.

Apparently, Michelangelo was a sucker for a bad piece of rock. His Medici Madonna is considered one of the most famous pieces of the sculptor's work, but the Madonna and Child broke midway through the carving process.

Just think about having invested so much time and creativity into a piece. You think it's coming along nicely, and then you concentrate on a feature of the face or on the arm. As you set mallet to hammer, you pound into a flaw—and the whole upper corner of the marble crumbles onto the floor.

Since Michelangelo had hand-cut the marble block himself, he must have felt like pounding the mallet into his own head. How could he have missed this flaw? He was creating the piece based on a prepaid commission, so he had a budget and a deadline to meet. Now what was he to do?

His original design consisted of the Child in a position looking over his mother's shoulder while she cuddled him. So Michelangelo made adjustments. He bent Mary's right arm around and behind her. He tilted her head to a place where he had enough stone to create it. He turned baby Jesus so he was clambering for his mother, squirming in her lap.

The sculpture was so far removed from what Michelangelo initially had in mind that he didn't finish it but left it unsanded. The marks from his rasps still show in the stone. Yet today, it's considered his greatest masterpiece. The tension created by moving that arm and then turning the Child in his mother's lap gives the piece a vitality and emotional energy seldom achieved in stone.

Do the creative misadventures of David and the Madonna and Child sound familiar? Sometimes it feels like someone is swinging a mallet our way! But then we turn around and see that it's our loving Lord at work. He carefully selects his material and sets to work, chiseling and shaping us into his image.

Yet, like Michelangelo, God is dealing with flawed stone. (Ain't that the truth!) Sometimes we crack and drop off chunks under the hands of the Artist. At times, he encourages us to take a certain position, but we bend our heads in stubborn resistance. Other times, little rivulets of imperfections show up as God works on us. So what does he do? Toss out our rocklike souls? No, he works around our hard heads and stony hearts to make us into something remarkable.

OK, so maybe my cracks are more like ravines. Maybe I'm more of a little chip off the old block than I'd like to admit. Maybe my stubbornness is greater than I'd care to own. In Isaiah 30:13, God likens our willful ways to being like a crack in a high wall that causes a bulge, and then suddenly the wall collapses. Yep, that's me.

But the other day, I heard about a dog named Clancy, whose stubbornness puts my mulish ways in the shadows. The puppy decided to dig in his paws over lots of issues when he was being trained, but what really did him in was the leash. As it was first introduced to him, Clancy suspiciously sniffed it. He eyed it. He decided he didn't like it.

But his owner, Marylee, clamped the leash onto his collar and set out on a walk. Clancy reluctantly followed. After a few yards of being tugged along, Clancy declared himself unwilling to move forward by lying down on his back and putting his legs up in the air.

At first hopeful that this was a sign of surrender, Marylee rubbed the dog's proffered pink tummy and cooed at him. Then she stepped out, assuming Clancy would right himself and trot along. Nope. Clancy just laid on his back. Marylee pulled on the leash. Clancy didn't move.

Realizing her dog had turned into a prone pillar, Marylee determined that her will would win the day. So she dragged Clancy down the dirt trail. (Don't call the animal rights folks, please. He wasn't hurt, I promise! Just keep reading.)

A few feet of digging a trench with his back convinced Clancy that resistance was futile. Thus, Clancy and Marylee completed their first walk. Marylee felt triumphant, and Clancy felt . . . well, it's hard to say, but we do know he was a lot dirtier than when the walk started. And eventually, as Marylee was happy to report, Clancy came to realize the leash meant an adventure was in the offing—but that was many months after he literally drew a line in the "sand" of a hiking trail.

I'm consoled to think that God is mindful of my quirky, chiseled-in-stone, stubborn ways. The Lord, unlike Michelangelo, isn't surprised when a chunk of me can't withstand life's blows. Like Michelangelo, God knows how to make the best of the material at hand and manages to create something out of so little.

We may not end up with a smooth sheen like David or the vivid interplay of the Madonna and Child, but the Master Sculptor has a "marked" effect on us. While life may not be all it's cracked up to be, God manages to make something beautiful out of it—often to our surprise.

*Master Sculptor, thank you for seeing us for the flawed beings we are. Thank you for not demanding perfection of us. We appreciate your willingness to work with us despite our hard heads and hearts. Help me to be willing to let you have a free hand with my life. And thank you for being inventive with me and persevering even when I resist.*

## Cracked-Up Questions

**In what ways has God been chiseling at your life?**

**Would you describe yourself as malleable or as resistant? Why?**

**How do you express yourself when you feel as though you'll crack under pressure (e.g., crying, pouting, yelling at God)?**

**Tell about a time you "pulled a Clancy."**

**What can you do to assist rather than resist the Sculptor's work in your life?**

# 19

# Word Explosions

*News flash! Patsy Clairmont died.*

Nobody was more surprised than I to hear about my death. When my daughter-in-law received a call asking if I had passed away, she assured the caller that I was alive and kicking. I was grateful this woman called to verify the claim and didn't spread the rumor by passing on her "news."

Mark Twain, who was also once presumed dead, quipped, "The report of my death was highly exaggerated."

How do rumors start? We misunderstand, jump to conclusions, or maybe just like to rock the boat. As we have all experienced, words are explosive enough to ruin reputations, to end friendships, or to prejudice minds. Words are also commanding enough to challenge a life, to convey love, and to initiate peace.

We've all heard someone say, "Oh, they made me feel so special." Or, "I felt like an intruder, so unwelcome." We can convey hostility or hospitality in a single syllable.

Perhaps it's their power that makes me so fascinated with words. Or maybe it's because I have so many words crowded inside of me just chomping to make themselves known.

Speaking of chomping, if I could eat the dictionary and digest all that verbiage, I would, and I believe it would be a delicious menu. Oh, some of them I would choose not to use, but having the right word at the right time is exhilarating. Proverbs 25:11 puts it this way: "A word fitly spoken is like apples of gold in settings of silver." Think of it: our words have the potential to be beautiful and valuable when well placed.

Now here's my current dilemma. At my age, I'll often be in the middle of a sentence only to lose my words, as if some intruder broke in and stole my golden apple. I know what I want to say, but I can't haul it up out of the cistern it has fallen into. I can see shiny vowels and glistening consonants wedged down in there, but I can't seem to bring them collectively to the surface. It takes three of my friends just to help me talk. Sometimes, we look like a pantomime show trying to act out our next word in hopes someone in the group will guess it. They're not necessarily chunky words with tons of syllables; why, I lose even petite treasures.

I know this is somewhat normal for my juncture in life, because I have had to help my friends talk as well. In fact, it's kind of fun; if one of us can tell a whole story without help, we applaud—for the story and for the burst of fluidity.

I also collect words, rather like my teacups and milk bottles. I find they come in handy in a tight Scrabble game. So to lose them is disconcerting.

I'm beginning to see that there's a reason *pause* dominates the word *menopause*; it's all part of the same package. It wouldn't feel so bad if I could eventually get over these mental speed bumps in my brain like one might recover from the measles, but the journeyers ahead of me on life's path claim it only gets worse. Which means pretty soon I'll be speaking Morse code—all dots and dashes. Of course, I always wanted to speak a second language . . .

Longtime friends tell me I'm much quieter than I used to be, and Les seconds that. Perhaps that's good. No, actually it is *very* good. For one thing, I needed some balance, since I was a habitual talker. I had to face that my need to constantly converse had to do with my need to be the center of attention. Life had become too much about me. I gradually learned that not all my thoughts needed to be unloaded into the atmosphere; we have enough pollution.

My friend's husband used to tell her, "When you're talking, you're not learning anything new." That observation stuck in my mind and helped me to let go of some of my words to make time for someone else's. In doing so, I have been amazed at how interesting other people's lives are.

As a former "big talker," I had often been a contributor to farfetched news. But now that I'm taking time to listen, I'm learning a lot more about what is really true after all.

*Lord, I am grateful that we can change. Rescue us from our words, or more precisely, from the things that need not be said. Keep us from idle chatter and nattering nonsense. And, if we lose our words, may the ones that remain be Savior-seasoned. Help the fruit of our lips to be gold and silver. May we make kindness and truth our dictionary, and may the Holy Spirit be our English instructor. Amen.*

## Cracked-Up Questions

**What has been said to you that made you feel welcomed or rejected?**

**Has something you've said been misunderstood? How did that make you feel?**

**Whose words have added strength and dignity to your life?**

**Generally speaking, during a conversation, do you talk more or listen more?**

**Are you a "big talker"? If so, why?**

# 20

# Puzzled

As a child, my first map was a United States picture puzzle, which proved to be prophetic. Today, maps remain a puzzle to my one-lane brain. (And, may I say many seasons later, hot flashes have not enhanced my directional deficiency. Actually, the heat has turned what little internal compass I had to soot.) I've never had a sense of north, south, east, and west—which has left me with a lifelong dependency on right, left, up, and down.

Folks who say things like, "It will be on the northeast corner" rankle me. They might as well have said, "Xyght rgmklz xy dl." In my color-coded mind, what I need someone to say is, "There will be a Big Lots on the corner, sporting orange letters. Turn left, go three miles until you see a neon sign flashing Stinky's, turn right, count five houses down, and turn left into the driveway with the purple-striped mailbox." Now those, honey, are directions.

In the mid-1700s, European mapmakers pasted maps onto wood and cut them into small pieces, which began jigsaw puzzles. The dissected map has been an educational toy ever since.

I remember as a kid making my own puzzles using movie stars' pictures out of magazines. I'd paste the picture on cardboard and then draw puzzle-shaped pieces on the picture and cut them out. No wonder I did poorly in geography. They should have asked me what movies Debbie Reynolds starred in, where John Wayne lived, or what hit song Tommy Sands recorded. Now, if those questions had been on the test, I'd have aced it.

Yesterday, I took a four-hour road trip with my friends Luci and Mary. What fun! Not only because these gals are delightful, but also because I didn't have to drive or read a map, which meant that if we got lost, it wasn't my fault.

As we headed out, Luci held the list of directions, which had been broken down into twelve steps guaranteed to lead us to our destination. Luci and Mary served as part-time drivers and co-pilots, while my job was to sit in the backseat and be cute. (Somebody's got to do it, so I volunteered!)

On the way there, we only made one wrong turn, and it was easily corrected. I personally call that a whopping success. But the trip home presented us with more than enough fodder to humble our big success story. Our problems began almost immediately and continued until we stumbled our way into the hotel where we were staying. I think the difficulty came from trying to reverse everything on the direction sheet. The curves to the right were now curves to the left, north was south, and east was west. It sounds simple, but at night, in unfamiliar territory, on back roads, while tired—well, let's just say that falling face-first into our pillows sounded redemptive.

My contribution during our lostness was occasionally to grunt in agreement or disagreement with their navigational suggestions. Quite honestly, I never had a clue where we were. I wasn't even doing that good a job at being cute.

I wonder if my map bewilderment came from my dad. It wasn't that he couldn't read a map; he just chose not to, because he was certain that, if you kept going, you would eventually find what you were looking for. Right.

We were on vacation in Kentucky, where Dad was born and raised, headed for my aunt's house, when Dad remembered a shortcut. Yep, you know what that means. When the road narrowed to two ruts, we knew we were lost. We wobbled over a single-lane wooden bridge that hadn't been used for eons, and finally we ended up parked next to an abandoned mine. We would still be driving, but Dad ran out of road. I laughed so hard I hurt.

Little did I realize the last laugh would be on me, as I've spent a lifetime directionally muddled. Actually, I prefer to say, as Robert Frost did, "I'm not confused; I'm just well-mixed."

We are all travelers, whether we want to be or not. Life forces us to hit the road in search of doctors, banks, dry cleaners, groceries, and many other things. Les and I divide our time between Texas and Michigan, which means for me, a non-mapper, that I seldom know where I am, much less where the bank is in relationship to our home. So sweet Les, in an attempt to simplify my perpetual lostness, chose the bank directly across the street from our subdivision. No missing piece there—out the driveway, into the bank. Now, if only life were that simple!

Thank heavens for Jesus, who offers to walk with us

wherever we are. He promises to guide our steps and light our path. Jesus is there for us if, like Zacchaeus, we are out on a limb. He's there for us if, like Eve, we've taken the wrong path. He's there for us if we are wandering aimlessly or high-stepping with certainty.

Jesus never loses sight of us, even when we're feeling hopelessly lost. He holds all our puzzle pieces. What looks broken to us is whole to him, because he is the beginning and the end of all things.

Whew!

*Lord, how grateful we are that you know not only our current location but also our final destination. You are our map and our compass. You make our crooked roads straight. We will follow you and you only, our Global Guide. Amen.*

## Cracked-Up Questions

**What was your first introduction to maps?**

**How well does your internal compass function?**

**What puzzles you about God?**

**Are there any missing puzzle pieces in your life?**

# 21

# Cruisin'

My friends Alan and Ginny met on a *Semester at Sea* cruise ship. Both were students on a four-month journey to faraway places. Isn't that romantic?

Well, actually, they met in Morocco in a bazaar that Ginny and her friend had entered to look around. Once inside, the owner wouldn't let the young women leave. The man began to intimidate and frighten the women, and then Alan strolled in and saw the girls' distress. Even though he didn't know them, Alan stepped in and peacefully rescued them. As you can imagine, Ginny and her friend were very grateful to this good Samaritan.

Back on board, Ginny couldn't get her mind off her fair-haired rescuer. She wanted to find a way to express her gratitude in a tangible way, when an idea came to her. At the next port, Ginny bought scrapbook supplies and filled the album with notes, poems, and pictures that she collected during the next thirteen weeks of their journey.

After that first encounter, Ginny and Alan met for meals

and then outings, including motor-scooter jaunts throughout South Africa, camel rides in India, elephant rides in Sri Lanka, and a safari in Africa. Ginny found Alan's friendly manner and playful humor winsome. Alan found Ginny's dark beauty and gentle manner pleasing. They shared a sense of adventure and a love for God. How romantic . . . Well, almost.

Even romance has its cracks. It turned out Alan had a serious relationship with someone else. Uh-oh. Poor Ginny . . . she was smitten. Poor Alan . . . he was confused. Poor Alan's girlfriend . . . she had no idea that a kind deed had sparked new love.

At the close of the cruise, Ginny gave Alan the scrapbook of their shared memories, and he was stunned. He had never received such a personal gift, designed just for him. He was deeply moved, but the time had come for them to go their separate ways. Ginny wondered if they would ever see each other again. Oh, heartache . . . Well, almost.

After months of emotional wrestling and heart searching, Alan realized he cared deeply for Ginny and didn't want to live without her. Following a tearful breakup with his girlfriend, Alan found Ginny, and their love blossomed into marriage. Aww!

Five years after they married, Alan and Ginny decided to take another *Semester at Sea* cruise. But this time, instead of going as students, they went as resident assistants overseeing one hundred of the five hundred students aboard. They decided to take Alan's beloved album so they could add pages to it and one day show their children the journey of their love story. How romantic . . . Well, almost.

When the story of Alan and Ginny's romance reached the ship's doctor, he asked to peruse their album. They were delighted to share their pictures, but then someone stole it from the doctor's quarters. Alan was beside himself; the album was his most prized possession.

A search was made, but the book didn't surface. Signs were posted, announcements made, and prayers offered, but to no avail. When the cruise came to an end and they were disembarking, Alan couldn't believe God hadn't answered his heartfelt cries. Then, just as he and Ginny were going through customs, Alan turned and said, "Ginny, I'll be back soon." Ginny watched as Alan hustled away, unwilling to let go of his lost book. How sad . . . Well, almost.

Alan made his way to the back of the cruise ship and knelt down on the fantail to pray one last time. When he had pled his heart, he turned to stand up. That's when his eye caught something atop one of the many garbage dumpsters holding the trash of more than one thousand passengers—his album. He ran down to customs, where Ginny was waiting, his face streaked with tears, embracing their storybook. Aww.

Alan and Ginny have now been married for thirty-seven years, and they have four treasured children, three adored grandchildren, and one much-worn album of priceless memories.

Now that's romantic!

*Lord, we are grateful that you are our good Samaritan. We understand that you rescued us from the intimidation of our sinful hearts. We had no way of escape until you delivered us out of the hand of the enemy. Our hearts are yours . . . forever. And thank you that you guide us to our mate, even if we have to travel around the world to meet him! Amen.*

## Cracked-Up Questions

**Share a love story from your life.**

**Tell about someone you have rescued.**

**Tell about a time someone rescued you.**

**What is your most prized possession?**

**What recent prayer has God answered in your life?**

## Chin Up

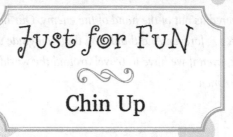

I was strolling inside my home (my idea of aerobics) when I passed the kitchen door and was startled by a bird on the lawn that was taller than I was. I thought that was rude. Now, granted, I'm not that tall—but then, most birds I know aren't either. In fact, most of the feathered friends that visit my yard would fit in my hand; so this one stopped me in my tracks.

She was from the heron family, with a long beak, skinny wading legs, and an extended neck. And what a neck it was . . . Why, she must get hungry just waiting for her food to make the slide down that endless funnel.

Unlike my bird friend, I have very little neck left because of the many chins that now ripple down like a wave pool. I'm not sure when they appeared, but I awoke one morning, and I didn't know which chin to rest in my hand.

I've learned to appreciate turtleneck shirts because they offer a garage for chins. Think about it. They keep those chins warm in the winter and, more importantly, keep them tucked out of sight. The problem is I now have so many little chins I have to pull up the turtleneck and clip it to my earrings just to contain them all. My latest challenge is to find a turtleneck bathing suit, preferably with sleeves and leggings. There must have been a run on them, because I could find nary a one.

What is all that sloppy soft stuff anyway? I think I know; it's brain cells. Honest. I read somewhere that, after you turn forty, ten thousand brain cells die daily. Well, they have to go somewhere, don't they? Mine apparently stockpiled in my neck to form chins.

A friend told me her leftover brain cells are flopping around her underarms. And another friend suggested that hers must have traveled to her bottom. I'm not sure cells could drop that far or sit that soft! But if they can, that may also explain my swollen feet.

Golly, just think of all those poor gals who had their extra chins siphoned off to look more youthful. One flush, and there went their brains.

The next time someone asks you, "Where are your brains?" just point to wherever yours are stockpiling, and smile pretty. (My mom told me if you don't have brains, you had better have a good smile.)

# 22

# Roadways

I first overheard Aunt Ada's name in occasional family conversations. Her name would be tossed into the exchange the way that people might mention a restaurant they once visited—casually, incidentally, and never in detail. Through childhood eavesdropping and connecting the dots, I learned she was my dad's sister who had died as a young adult before I was born. As time went by, I saw a picture of her. Ada appeared sad, frail, and faraway. She looked like a person who might have been instead of one who was.

I was an adult before I asked my grandmother about Aunt Ada. Grandma told me my aunt had died of a broken heart. Now, I had heard of people dying of broken hearts, but I didn't think it really happened. And I surely didn't know I was related to someone who had.

For some reason, as an adult, I ended up with several of Ada's possessions: a fountain pen, an ink bottle, a sketch, photographs, and a necklace. I could hold my aunt's belongings in one hand. Not much to represent an entire life.

Even though I know so little about her, Aunt Ada often crosses my mind. I've wondered about her heartache, her relationship with Christ, how we would have gotten along, and if we had any similar attributes.

I presume Ada liked to sketch, since I have one of her drawings hanging near my desk. My dad sketched as well; actually, we called his art "doodling." Most of Dad's markings took place on napkins and his newspaper's borders. His graphite strips reminded me of cave drawings. Often his subjects were Boxer dogs, cartoonish people, and bushy trees. I, too, enjoy pushing a pencil, but my art attempts would be defined more as passionate scribbling.

It makes me giggle that all three of us—Dad, Aunt Ada, and I—shared an interest we weren't any good at. Our renderings were more like fidgety pastimes. Somewhere in our heritage, a real artist must lurk; but all our artistic ancestor passed through the gene pool was desire.

Ada's necklace is a frail chain with a bone-colored tiny monocle that, when held up to your eye, allows you to view a small, magnified print of the Lord's Prayer. I wondered how important the necklace was to my aunt. Or if it was something that survived the years because she never wore it. Maybe her parents had given it to her. Or her lost love. Then again, it may have been a prize from Sunday school for winning the Bible drill. I'll never know for sure, but I'd like to believe it was a treasure she prized.

The man who broke her heart married someone else. I wondered how he felt when he heard of Ada's passing. I feel bad when I hear an "enemy" has died, much less a former sweetheart, so I imagine it saddened him.

In my stack of old photographs are some from the cemetery the day Aunt Ada was buried. I can see pain in the pictures of those who came to mourn her passing, especially in my grandparents' sad eyes. From that day forward, they, too, had broken hearts. I heard it, even as a child, in my grandmother's crackly voice when she spoke of Ada. I have no recollection of my grandfather's voice, because he seldom spoke when I was growing up. I wondered if his heart hurt too much to talk.

The ink sketch I have of Aunt Ada's is one of a dusty road. I've wondered where the road led. To her former sweetheart? To a better day? To a new love? Perhaps to a heavenly home?

Long ago and far away, two men traveled by foot on a dusty road. As they walked, they were deep in conversation about someone they knew, a teacher. They had heard of him in the conversations of others in the villages, and as time went on, more and more stories of him were exchanged among the townspeople. Finally, these men were drawn into his company and followed his teachings.

But this day, the men spoke of his shocking crucifixion. He had left behind a handful of stories, promises, and unanswered questions. Their expectations were dashed. Great mystery surrounded this teacher as they spoke of his intentions and his resulting death. It was said he died of a broken heart—a heart broken for humankind.

They wondered aloud about him. They had many stories—and what stories they were!—of water dripping into wine, lepers leaping whole, bread feeding thousands, Pharisees scoffing, and now a crushing crucifixion. What did it all mean?

A thousand thoughts whirled through their minds as they chattered on. In fact, they were so caught up in their questions that they hardly noticed that the Answer had joined them on their journey. Until he spoke . . . and their hearts burned within them. What man is this? They took a second look. Then their eyes were opened. It was Jesus, the risen Savior (Luke 24:13–35).

Consider this: the Jesus who revealed himself to those men walks with us today on our road of wondering and contemplating. The road of trying to figure out what he has said and what he is doing in our lives. The place where we wrestle with what we believe and what has transpired. On our journey, we, like the disciples on the Emmaus Road, can become so engrossed with our surmising that we miss Jesus's clear presence.

Fortunately, he has left more than a few trinkets behind to help us know him.

*Lord, inflame our hearts that we might know you for who you are, the risen Christ who walks with us and talks with us. Silence our frantic conversations of worry over your holy workings. Cause us to rest in your unfolding plans. Sit down with us, break bread, and bless it, that our eyes might see and our minds might grasp that being in your presence is the answer. We magnify your name. Amen.*

## Cracked-Up Questions

What attributes do you share in common
with other family members?

What handful of remnants are you leaving behind?

Who has dashed your expectations?

How often do others hear you speak of Jesus?

When was the last time your heart burned within you?

# 23

# Say What?

The other day, I was reading my dictionary. I did mention I love words, didn't I? I mean, you never know when you might find the perfect word that would enable you to use all your Scrabble tiles in one smooth move. Anyway, while roaming around in my dictionary, I came across the word *crack-jaw.* No, it isn't a synonym for jawbreakers. It refers to a word that is hard to pronounce.

You know, like those names you come across in the Bible such as Mephibosheth. It's tough even finding a nickname for such a guy! (Phibo?) Or the word Jesus uttered to heal a deaf-mute: *ephphatha*. I'd end up just spitting syllables if I tried to say that one.

Benjamin Disraeli, who was a pretty bright guy—a novelist, debater, and prime minister of England—tried to identify a person once and ended up exclaiming, "A Polish nobleman, a Count somebody; I never can remember their crack-jaw name." And I thought menopause was the reason I was pausing over people's names . . . sometimes including my own, but here's a new excuse for my mental pause.

Lots of folks I know have developed crack-jaw names in the last few years. I've never considered my name crack-jaw, but I do remember one day someone else found it so. I was just beginning to come out of my agoraphobic days and had surprised myself by agreeing to do a book review in front of several hundred women at a conference. I was a nervous Nellie, which manifested itself in a variety of ways. I could hardly sit still and kept flipping through my note cards like they were a deck of bridge cards. Why, I could barely breathe. I was sure I couldn't walk to the podium, let alone utter a word (*crack-jaw!*) should I manage to remain standing once I got onstage.

Then I heard the person introduce me as Clutsy Pairmount. The women erupted in laughter. Somehow their response to the silly name was like a shot of adrenaline. I rushed up front and started chattering away. First thing I knew, it was all over, and everyone seemed to have enjoyed the reviews. Thank God for the emcee's crack-jaw moment!

I've found that most of us have trouble pronouncing certain words. As a matter of fact, the other day I found a list of the one hundred most frequently mispronounced words. I noticed a few that I've been slaughtering but also saw several that surprised me. Some folks are really confused by English. Here's a sampling:

"A blessing in disguise" is referred to by some as "a blessing in the skies." "Chest of drawers" is believed to be "chester drawers." "Dog-eat-dog world" becomes "doggy-dog world"—

which is a whole lot nicer but is pretty raucous with all that barking and sniffing. "Duct tape" is considered to be "duck tape" by some. I've never found a need to tape a duck, but my furnace ducts respond well to a bit of tape. The "Heimlich maneuver" is often pronounced "Heineken remover," which is also a possibility, although the goal is to save the life of someone choking on a bit of food rather than a method to remove beer from a saturated drinker. Then there's real confusion when someone is trying to establish "law and order," but listeners hear "Laura Norder," whoever she might be. Talk about communication breakdowns!

I also found out that the word *appendicitis* was considered so crack-jaw in 1885 that it was left out of the biggest, most thorough dictionary of the English language, *The Oxford English Dictionary,* which requires a magnifying glass to read it's so big. But then, in 1902, Edward VII's coronation was postponed because he needed his appendix removed. Suddenly *appendicitis* wasn't crack-jaw anymore, and it's now a commonly understood word—although perhaps only Scrabble players and doctors know how to spell it.

Speaking of spelling, Jewish scholars at one point chose not to spell out God's name because they considered it too sacred to write each letter. They chose to view the name as crack-jaw—they wouldn't pronounce it, because to utter the word would be to profane it. The Jewish readers of Scripture believed they were too broken, too mundane, to write or to say that name.

So they substituted the Hebrew word for "my Lord" in all the places where the holy name appeared (without all its letters). Then they combined the vowels from the Hebrew "my Lord" with the consonants of the holy name to come up with the name "Jehovah."

While I appreciate such reverence, I like to think about God as expressed in John 1:1: "In the beginning was the Word, and the Word was with God, and the Word was God." So God was a Word? I suspect that means he was without physical form as we think of it; he was more of an entity—and a very complex one at that.

John goes on to say, "He was in the beginning with God. All things were made through Him, and without Him nothing was made that was made. In Him was life, and the life was the light of men. And the light shines in the darkness, and the darkness did not comprehend it" (vv. 2–5).

I have often felt crack-jaw when I try to comprehend God. But to think of him as a Word, a powerful bundle of complexity that created everything, really does leave me speechless, which is a condition I'm not used to. Imagine such a Word! It would contain the essence of being, the founder of life, and even the spark of light.

Yet the book of Acts tells us how approachable God is: "Those among you who fear God, to you the word of this salvation has been sent" (13:26). Now, with this I can relate. Jesus, the Word, is my salvation. My Savior wrapped flesh around his powerful, complex self so I could touch him, comprehend his closeness, and receive salvation by—of all things—saying his name.

That is such good news that it leaves me crack-jaw!

*God of all words, thank you that you sought us and assumed our humble form so that we can more perfectly understand your nature. Thank you that, despite your holiness, you have made yourself known to us. Help us to always revere you but never to feel that we can't approach you. Help us to form the words necessary to speak to you, our Father.*

## Cracked-Up Questions

**Tell about a person whose name you have had trouble pronouncing. How did you deal with it? How did he or she?**

**What does your name mean to you?**

**What names do you use when you pray to God? Why are these favorites?**

**What name for God comforts you most?**

**When you feel too broken to relate to God, what about him helps you to overcome your hesitation?**

## 24

# Weighty Matters

Now I've heard it all! I know that we, the public, have proven ourselves vulnerable to scams, and I realize that the world is on a perpetual diet, but now we can laugh our weight off? I mean, what happened to the theory that round people are jovial? Did we pack that idea away with hula hoops and mood rings? Wouldn't all of us giddy, girthy girlfriends be the first to notice if we could chuckle till our buckle cinched?

According to some joyologists (uh-huh, *joyologists*—those given to the promotion of joy), you can lose weight if you guffaw daily. So does this mean we can titter till our tummies tuck? Or better yet, chortle till the cellulite runs smooth? I'm afraid I'd have to be permanently hysterical to accomplish that task.

Can't you see it now? A world emphasis on belly laughing, with people lining up single file around the block, waiting to slip into a joy booth so they can laugh off lunch. Or employers offering health incentives for workers who snicker heartily. Or etched joy lines on our countenance being applauded because they indicate our amiableness rather than our need for Botox.

We live in a "make me happy" and "make life easy" society. Our humor wanes when we are made to wait or wonder. And for heaven's sake, don't make us wonder. We have to know, and we have to know in a microwave moment.

But suppose you're not like I am. (How presumptuous of me to think you are!) Perhaps you love wondering and you are a superb waiter . . . Yeah, sure. Think about it. When was the last time you strummed your fingers on the counter because the microwave was too slow, the traffic light didn't turn quickly enough, the express lane doddered, your pastor preached too long, or your dog couldn't decide which blade of grass to water?

Waiting weighs. And wondering—well, it's downright pudgy with pressure. I want to know where all the boats and airplanes disappeared to in the Bermuda Triangle. Don't you? What really happened to Amelia Earhart? I know her plane went down, but where? And why are my thighs sticking out farther than my hips?

These things mystify me. I like the tidiness of a package with all the ribbons tied up in a bow. I despise "To be continued" in a series. I don't want to be left sitting on the edge of my chair. I like resolution. Not knowing doesn't tickle me; not a solitary giggle will come forth from my anatomy when I'm left to stew.

Have you ever wondered why God designed us with the ability to laugh and to cry? I guess he knew we would need to do both as a way to pour off emotional excess; otherwise, we might blow a gasket. And gasket blowing is so untidy.

I've heard it said that hearty laughter sends fresh shipments of oxygen to the brain, which causes it to loosen up. Hmm, if it can loosen up my brain, then maybe, just maybe, the joyologists are right, and it could loosen up my jeans. That would be great. Then I wouldn't have to unsnap them to eat, sit, travel, and breathe.

I'd much rather chuckle myself fit than deny myself indulgences, but I have this nagging feeling I may need to do both.

*Lord, thank you for the relief that comes with laughter. May waiting and wondering not knock the humor out of us, but instead may they cause us to trust you regarding the future you have prepared for us. You are our joyologist; you give us reason to laugh aloud. I love to hear my children's laughter, which makes me believe our joyous responses bring you pleasure. How delightful. Amen.*

## Cracked-Up Questions

**When was the last time you made others laugh really hard?**

**What or who makes you laugh?**

**How well do you wait?**

**What do you wonder about?**

**What tiny thoughts are in your repertoire?**

## *Just for FuN*

### Cell-U-Photo. Huh?

My friend Ginger is a multitasker and therefore loves superstores that enable her to do a gazillion things in her one-stop-shopping effort. The other day, she cruised into the store with her to-do list and ticked off her accomplishments: order son's contact lenses, drop off film to be developed, pick up a few grocery items, and grab a quick hot dog at the café for lunch. Whew! She had done it in record time and now could continue on to yet other destinations.

Ginger was off and running to pick up her son at school when she remembered she needed to call her husband at work. Reaching into the folds of her purse, she pulled forth . . . a handful of film. Initially confused and believing she had left the film at the store, she fished back in her purse and came forth with more film. That's when it hit her: she had deposited her cell phone in the photo drop-off slot and then put the film in her purse. Oops.

Ginger cracked up and continued tittering all the way back to the store. (So much for record time.) When she arrived there, she asked the salesclerk if she had found the phone, and then Ginger proceeded to explain her absentminded mistake.

The gal proclaimed, "Thank heavens you're back. I've been trying for thirty minutes to figure out how to get the pictures out of your phone!"

Ginger giggled enough over that incident that she worked off the hot dog. And she's probably out multitasking even as I write. She's my kind of girlfriend.

## 25

# Tweedle Dee, Tweedle Dum

What do you do when you get restless? Frayed nerves have a way of shaking out their tension in individual antics.

My dad was a thumb twirler, a change rattler, a finger thumper, a whittler, and a whistler.

My mom sang, especially during storms, tidied the house incessantly, crocheted passionately, and bounced her foot until the china in the nearby cabinet wobbled.

My grandma wrung her willowy hands, fiddled with the tatting on her handkerchief until it was tattered, and rocked in her creaky rocker until it almost drove others off theirs.

I chew gum aggressively, pace annoyingly, shop often, eat more often, and play computer Scrabble in sporadic fits.

It's only human to channel our nervous energies into a habit. We all have our reactions to tension. Life can be stressful, and some folks' way of dealing with it is to sink down so deeply in a chair that you need a forklift to pry them out. Others leap up and race hither and yon like nervous Nellies.

You couldn't get them to sit still for two minutes if you hog-tied them! We are all wired differently, and what bugs one of us may not be an issue for someone else.

I can't stand even a grain of sand in my shoe. So you can imagine how stressed I would have been hiking the desert with Moses for forty years. And my husband would have gone bonkers if his menu was limited to manna.

Of course, the Israelites didn't have much choice, did they? And sometimes stressors are relative. I mean, next to the cruel labor requirements that they suffered in Egypt, what's a little sand between one's toes? And coming from a life of slavery in a strange land, what's a restricted menu, especially if you are headed toward freedom and a land flowing with milk and honey?

Today, we live in an indulgent era with menus galore. We have commercialism, conveniences, and comforts from shore to neon-signed shore. We Americans enjoy pleasures aplenty. Or do we?

Oh, I know we have a lot, but I'm not certain how much pleasure we receive from our extras. For instance, how many times have you come home from a vacation exhausted, sunburned, and broke? Wouldn't it be easier to stay home, rest in the shade, and be financially solvent? I always think of that after a whirlwind trip has whittled five years off my life expectancy and put a crimp in my retirement fund.

Or have you ever looked forward to a day at a theme park only to find you spent 60 percent of the time standing in long lines with overwrought, overstimulated children who needed a nap? Then add to the headache of the parents the drain of repeatedly trying to convince little ones of how much fun they are having.

Or perhaps you took your boat to the lake only to get caught in traffic, ticketed for not hooking up both brake lights, bitten by a passel of obnoxious mosquitoes, and frustrated when the boat motor froze in the middle of the lake and you had to paddle back to shore using a bait bucket. Those types of kinks in our plans can inspire twitches to appear in our eyebrow, cause a herd of hives to erupt, and produce a soured disposition.

Have you ever eaten yourself into a stupor? Purchased items you didn't need? Or worked yourself to a frazzle? Me too.

"Less is more" has become a popular mantra in our society. I'm not convinced it has caught on in actuality, but it does have heads nodding in agreement. It's as if the bobbing of our noggins makes us appear savvy, but in truth many of us continue to live stuck in the muck of plenty. For instance, a second vehicle, as convenient as it is, requires insurance, maintenance, and pricey gas. It takes up valuable space in the garage and driveway, and it's always parked in the wrong spot when you need it. It competes for space with other vehicles littering our lots: bicycles, motorbikes, and motorized lawn equipment. Is it worth the hassle and frustration?

I'm starting to sense that many of our itches, twitches, lumps, and bumps may be brought on by our own choices to dive into society's pool of muchness. We sometimes need to be reminded what a worthy use of our time backyard gardening is, how rejuvenating a swing in the hammock can be, how relaxing a good read is, and how invigorating it is to stroll through our own neighborhood. Those would be upgraded choices from tension headaches and mysterious blotches that surface with a jammed calendar.

I'm not so naive as to believe that if we trimmed back on indulgences we wouldn't have tension. I just wonder if we we're not adding unnecessary pressure to our already challenging stint here on earth with our pleasure-seeking, stuff-gathering tendencies.

*Lord, teach us the simple life. We don't want to be so encumbered we spend all our energies in the wrong places. Help us to own our nervous behaviors and make necessary adjustments. We don't want to just switch our outside behavior, but we want to resolve, with your help, our inside conflict. We need our frayed nerve-endings knit back into place, something we acknowledge only you can do. In the midst of our challenging lives, cause us to be wise enough to make you our number one priority. Amen.*

## Cracked-Up Questions

What nervous behavior do you exhibit that reveals your anxiety level?

When stressed, do you sit down or speed up?

Which of your pleasures have turned to hassles?

List any indulgences you should rein in.

Define your picture of the simple life.

What can you realistically change to simplify?

# 26

# In the Fine Print

Recently, as I sat in a hotel restaurant, I watched a worker move purposefully about her tasks. She refilled containers on the buffet line, cleaned up the waffle station, and returned pans stacked higher than her head to the kitchen. As she scurried about, she never smiled, and she appeared to be put out. I had the distinct feeling someone hadn't come in for his shift, and I was sure these tasks were outside her job description.

I identify. So often life serves up hassles I didn't sign up for. I sometimes have thought, *Excuse me, where does it say I wanted this aggravation in my life?* Take Sylvia . . . please.

Sylvia didn't think my young son should ride his bicycle in front of our respective homes because his shaky, undeveloped skills made her nervous. My loving thought was, *Well then, don't look.* I didn't say that, but I thought it real loud. How else would my boy learn to ride his bike if we didn't give him an opportunity? Besides, if she didn't sit on her porch all day watching everything going on in the neighborhood, she wouldn't have to worry about what others were doing. As you can surmise, mercy is not my gift.

One day Sylvia planted some flowers in her front yard, which would seem friendly except that she crowded them right up next to our driveway. They were on her property, but I knew someone from my clan would eventually swerve a tire onto her pansies, making her furious. It was as if she had planted them in hopes they would bloom into a problem. And sure enough . . . they did. I ran over them. It happened so quickly, just a slight flinch of the steering wheel, that I didn't even realize I had squashed a patch of happy little flower faces until I disembarked from my car and encountered Sylvia's face, which was not happy. Let's just say I could be found after sunset, murmuring unpleasantries, on my knees next to a tray of flowers from our local nursery, repairing the breach.

Then my friend's Pekinese, Zippy, bolted from her car, dashed into Sylvia's yard, hiked his leg, and proceeded to water her begonias. My friend and I screamed, which only served to startle Zippy into a more sizable contribution. Not good, Zippy, not good.

This time I coerced my husband into shoveling us out of this mess with our neighbor. I didn't want to face Sylvia's scowling judgment or listen to her criticisms, especially while I did latrine labor.

Much to my chagrin, when Les came home, he said, "I think you may have our neighbor all wrong."

"Huh?" I asked, feeling an attitude coming on.

"Really. I chatted with her, and while she was displeased

with Zippy's uninvited appearance, I think her bigger issue is she's lonely."

"Well, no wonder," I spouted.

"She has no children, and she's been widowed for many years. Think about it, Patsy. How often do you see anyone visit her? Yep," Les said thoughtfully, "I think she needs a friend."

"Well, help yourself," I retorted. As I walked away, I grew a bit uncomfortable. But I pushed those feelings aside.

In the weeks ahead, my husband had chats over the back fence with Sylvia. He even gave her one of our extra nozzles to water her flowers, and then the man crossed a line. *My* line. Les invited her to join our family for a backyard picnic.

I wasn't happy, and he knew it. But the day before the picnic, everything changed. A vicious summer storm moved to our county, sending us not only indoors, but also to our basements. We listened to the wild winds beat against our home, and as we hunkered down for the heavy rains, we heard pounding. It took us a moment to realize someone was at our side door. Les disappeared up our steps and returned within minutes with—who else?—Sylvia.

"I'm afraid," she half-whispered through shaky lips. "May I join you until this passes?"

Something hard within me lost its tension. I hadn't really noticed that Sylvia was just a wisp of a woman, actually almost frail. I wondered how she pounded so loudly, as I looked at her thin frame. When I viewed her through my resentment, she had seemed sinister and wily. But now she just seemed vulnerable.

We waited out the storm together. Lightning cracked,

thunder roared, and the wind whipped at our roof tiles, sending some twirling around our neighborhood. And wouldn't you know it, a couple landed on Sylvia's prize roses.

When we walked outside to survey our homes, I braced myself. But instead of erupting when she spotted her crushed flowers, Sylvia helped us retrieve the tiles and then thanked us for sheltering her. Those were the first kind words I had heard her utter in the three years we had lived side by side.

That night as I prayed, I realized I had contributed to the friction between us. I had been defensive and in many ways more judgmental than she. I viewed everything she did as intentionally hostile, which I now realized was more about me than her.

In time, we developed a warm exchange. Sylvia still didn't want me to drive over her pansies, and I didn't blame her. But I found out she had planted them there as a neighborly gesture, not a means to create problems. I had seen that thoughtful effort through a smudged lens.

Yes, sometimes the very things I had thought outside of my job description—such as planting daisies at night and keeping Zippy off Sylvia's lawn—were actually divine assignments to save me from my myopic self.

*Lord, clear the smudges from our judgments, that we might realize we are all frail, faulty, and vulnerable. Help us to do whatever you give to us with a full heart. May you deliver us from thinking that anything you assign us is below our dignity. May we kneel in agreement with your plan and therefore rise in peace. Amen.*

## Cracked-Up Questions

When was the last time you felt life handed you something outside your agreed-on contract?

How did you respond?

How are you doing with your neighbors? Coworkers? Any you'd trade for a Pekinese?

How do judgments against others taint your view?

27

# Nut Crackin'

Drosselmeier, Marie's godfather in the classic story *The Nutcracker and the Mouse King,* tells little Marie a tale about Christian, a young lad who was turned into a nutcracker. The story goes that every hundred years the Nutcracker has a chance to break the curse and be changed back into a boy—but only if he can crack the hardest nut in the land.

When I read the story, the phrase "crack the hardest nut in the land," jumped off the page and yodeled my name. Why, I could be the poster girl for that nugget. Trust me, it takes more than a mild thud to press truth through my hard-shelled opinions.

The dictionary defines *opinion* as "a personal view." Now, the problem with looking at life solely from our own angle is that the viewing glass is cracked, causing a distorted perspective. Then, when we hear a statement that conflicts with our opinions, we react.

I'm naturally feisty. It's coded in my DNA, and I haven't appreciated it when folks mess with my thoughts. Why, I can get downright scrappy defending my stances, which is why it takes a two-edged sword to separate me from some of my wrong thinking.

In that way, I'm sort of like a Brazil nut, which hits the ground with such force that the pod could kill someone standing below. The natives use machetes to open the nuts and to remove the large seeds contained in each gigantic pod.

God's Word, that double-edged sword, can break into hard hearts and heads to get to the "seeds" of our fraudulent thinking. But sometimes we humans toss around our opinions and hurt those standing nearby.

Les and I have been tossing opinions at each other for years. Some of them hit with the force of hand grenades. When we look back now, we wonder why we would have used up all that youthful vigor on topics that didn't matter. Why would we spat over the "correct" way to hang toilet tissue, squeeze a toothpaste tube, park a car, make a bed, or fold a towel?

Wasn't that silly? I mean, whose life will it change if the tissue cascades off the top or unfurls from the bottom of the roll? Should a rumpled toothpaste tube ignite relational sparks? Of course not. (Today, we each have our own tube—his is tidier.) And what does it matter in the big scheme of life if my car looks more abandoned than parked? It has taken Les and me time to get over ourselves and to make room for more than our own way.

OK, OK . . . we're still working on it. Last weekend, Les and I locked horns. For our grandson's birthday, I bought him an educational game he really wanted. Les thought that a tad boring, so he bought him some tools, including a hacksaw.

Our grandson is five years old. The hacksaw sported a ten-inch carbon steel blade. I could just imagine him adjusting the height of the dining room table—or his younger brother. I won on that one . . . for now.

I wasn't as insightful with my son Marty. I believed all children should have music lessons. I always thought if I'd had piano lessons when I was young, I would have been happier. (As if pressing ivories was the secret to happiness!) So when my firstborn was old enough, I started him on piano with a private teacher. It didn't cheer him.

After a month, the teacher came to me and said, "Leave Marty alone. He wasn't meant to play an instrument." She was right. Marty was meant to disassemble motors, wire electrical systems, and do all types of installation work. (He's the one who should have had the hacksaw.) His music would come from the whir of smoothly running systems. I was trying to get Marty to march to the tune of my piano dreams rather than to the tune he was created to play.

That teacher rescued Marty from my musical opinion based on my distorted desire. The desire to play wasn't wrong, but forcing it on Marty wasn't the answer. And it was an injustice to a little tyke who had no interest or ear. God bless his teacher.

Of course, sometimes life's experiences are teachers in their own right. As a young adult, I was of the opinion that folks who grieved too long after the loss of a loved one weren't very spiritual. Then my only brother was killed in a car accident when he was thirty-eight years old. I was devastated. I grieved and grieved and grieved. In fact, if I think about it too long, even today, thirty years later, I can feel myself slide back into my loss.

What I've learned from grief is that it doesn't prevent me from being spiritual; it can, surprisingly, help me to clarify what I believe about God. Heartbreak opens us up, and in our vulnerability, we become acutely aware of our limitations. My perspective on grief is more compassionate today after my experience, and tender adjustments by God have helped me to see loss and hurting people differently.

In that way, I'm like a member of the cashew family. Ever wonder why cashews are shelled when we buy them? Think about it. Have you ever seen a cashew in its shell? Me neither. It turns out that a cashew has caustic oil between the nut's inner and outer shells. To rid this delectable treat of its acerbic element, the outer shell is burned or roasted off, and then the nut is boiled or roasted again to remove the inner shell.

Life's hardships often feel as though someone has turned up the heat on us, and we wonder if we'll survive. Yet I find when I've been "roasted" long enough in life's difficulties, my outer casing of bad attitudes, preconceived notions, and high-mindedness is burned off. I'm left meeker, less defensive, more pliable, and less caustic.

Remember young Christian, who longed to be a boy again but had to break the curse by cracking the hardest nut in the land? Here's our good news: Jesus has broken the curse of sin that rested upon us that we might be liberated people. He died for every "nut" in the land . . . even the hardest one. And for that, I'm particularly grateful.

*Lord, unshackle our hearts from hard-shell opinions that would encase us in acidic behavior. Remind us again that your ways always lead to our highest good. And thank you that we don't have to wait a hundred years to change, but we can begin today. Amen.*

## Cracked-Up Questions

What's the difference between an opinion and a belief?

What life experience changed your opinions?

Share a story from your life when you tried to engineer someone else's experiences.

In what ways might your perspective be distorted?

What do you think causes distortions?

What causes you to build your hard shell of defensiveness?

What are you defending? Pride? Rights? Reputation?

28

# From a High Perch

How long has it been since you sat and watched the world go by?

I mean that quite literally. As I write, I'm perched in a hotel window seat high above a major city's activity. I watch as waves of cars, buses, cabs, and limos pour through the streets, weaving and signaling their intentions. In the distance, I see an occasional horse-drawn carriage saunter through an intersection, followed soon after by a trolley that darts across toward its destination. Bicyclists with flashing lights on their backs pedal furiously amid the flow of vehicles, causing me to strain for their safety.

Foot traffic thrives in this city. Some folks—like the trolley—hurry with purpose, high-stepping at a fast pace, while others—like the carriages—amble, clomping along slowly. Six young men on skateboards push and glide in single file. From my perspective, they appear to be attached by cords as they gyrate their boards almost in unison. Families push baby carriages, couples stay close, and some folks tote chunky backpacks, which leaves me to wonder what burdens they are carrying.

The city is colorful with signal lights, neon signs, and fluttering, multicolored streamers that wave from narrow poles. But it's not the hustle, bustle, or flashy colors that capture my attention. Instead, it's the startling contrast of something happening directly below me.

Many stories down, children play in a multileveled catacomb composed of cement squares and rectangles; some form towers, and others descend into stairwells. A dozen children rush to enter the labyrinth, eager to repeatedly get lost and found. Squeals of delight waft in the air as they dash around the towers, sidestepping each other, looking for the perfect place of safety.

Nearby lies the contrast. A man in a dark hooded sweatshirt is stretched out on the cement, his head buried in the crook of his arm. He appears asleep—or maybe dead. A small bag containing his possessions is wedged strategically between him and a two-foot cement planter. His solitary form speaks volumes: he is alone, without any personal space or a private place to sleep. When did he stop caring who saw him sprawled out, or does he think no one notices?

The young ones are unaware of him, and he certainly doesn't respond to their presence. Years and pain separate them, yet they are only twenty feet apart. My view is different from theirs as I look down and see a picture of two worlds—frolicking youngsters and a destitute life.

Here is my pondering: How did the terrain of that man's life lead him to what appears to be a dead-end existence?

How did he go from being a playful child enthralled with hiding places to a pitiful form of one forgotten?

Or is he forgotten?

Perhaps he has a mom who kneels at her bedside at this very moment and cries out for God's mercy for her lost son. Or maybe his dad searches the streets, alleys, bars, and shelters in hopes of finding him . . . yet again. And then there's always the chance no one pursues him but God.

God has never lost track of him, no matter what park bench or Dumpster he chose to shelter in. Nor has the Holy One ceased to love him. Talk about contrast! The Lord will woo and wait for him as long as there is a pulse in that man's body. Redemption is as close as his next breath. One earnest heart cry and his world can change, crack open to new possibilities.

Evening has begun to creep into the city now, which causes the catacombs to empty. The children go to homes, families, and beds. The lost man staggers to his feet as if called by some distant drum and wanders off into the forming night until he becomes one more shadow in the distance.

I pray for him.

I may be one of many, or I may be the solitary soul God has assigned this night to the nameless man . . . the man who reminds me of my own ache of loneliness that sometimes creeps into my life in this crowded world.

*Lord, usually I am encircled with people caught up in a maze of activities, but tonight I'm alone, still, and observant. I forget how misguided a life can become . . . I forget what your grace rescued me from. Thank you that you continue to pursue lost lambs, even ones in a stupor. Make this man aware that you notice him, and intervene in his life. Until the day you take us home to heaven, may you keep us tender toward the destitute, downcast, disgusting, and the forgotten here on earth. Remind us often if necessary that we have been all those things, and you unreservedly drew us in close to your heart. Amen.*

## Cracked-Up Questions

**What do you learn as you watch people?**

**Are you a high-stepper or a clomper?**

**Who do you most identify with—the children or the hooded man? Why?**

**When you feel forgotten, who prays for you?**

# 29

# Egged On

My husband is a good egg. He tells a lot of yolks, he has a soft-boiled heart, and he's—what else?—all cracked up. Otherwise, we wouldn't be compatible.

Did you know that you can tell if an egg is raw or hard-cooked by spinning it? If the egg spins like a top, it's hard-cooked, but if it wobbles like a Weeble, it's raw. Try it.

Spinning people is far riskier. If they're raw, well, who knows what they might do? They could break open and slobber all over you. I hate when that happens. And if they're hard-cooked, all I can say is watch out when they run out of spin.

I personally am a conundrum. I am both hard and delicate (sounds better than "raw"). Perhaps that's true of most of us. We have our ornery times and our fragile moments. What time of the month it is, whether I like my job, and who is doing the spinning often determine my response. I become very Weeble-like (sounds better than "slobbering") when my nerves are frayed and my coping mechanisms are stretched rubber-band thin. After only a few turns, I'm all tears. I begin to crack, and then—oh dear, here it comes!—I slobber. Whereas, if I'm full of, say, my agenda and am pressed for time, then when you twirl into my space and set me in a spin, I can be hard-boiled. My shell thickens, and even the color of my yolk fades.

A yolk's color depends on the hen's diet. Add, say, a few marigolds to her feed, and her light yolks brighten up dramatically. Similarly, I find that if I've had a regular diet from the Scriptures, I'm not only brighter but I also handle an unexpected spin with greater finesse.

This is probably an apt moment to mention that in addition to collecting teapots and milk bottles, I'm also a chicken collector. I have, as my two-and-a-half-year-old grandson Noah says, "buk-buks" all over my house. I own some in porcelain and wood and even one prized bronze bird. I don't know what's up with this mild obsession with chickens. I wasn't raised on a farm, although when I was growing up, my mother frequently asked me if I was born in a barn. (I believe that had something to do with doors left ajar rather than her having forgotten where she gave birth to me, I think.)

I don't care for barns . . . too much fragrance and too many little creatures dashing about. But I enjoy watching chickens peck. I think it's dear to watch my friend's chickens meander about her property, bobbing their heads as they move into hunt-and-peck mode. I think I like "buk-buks" so much because I love breakfast, which brings us back to eggs.

Here's a little farmyard lore: A hen can produce a double-yolked egg, and on a rare occasion, a young hen can lay a yolkless one. That would be quite a surprise on a hungry morning. Not what one expects—but then again, life rarely is.

Take me, for instance. I never expected nine years after the birth of our first son to find out I was with "egg." We had resigned ourselves to one child when a new yolk hit town.

I had made a series of visits to the doctor as he tried to figure out why I was so sick and dropping weight. It never entered any of our minds that I was pregnant. I can still see my doctor, head bent over my files, shaking his head and saying, "I just don't know, Patsy. I just don't know."

Casually I said, "Doctor, I find it strange that I've lost all this weight and yet last week I had to buy a bigger bra."

His head popped up like a carnival duck at a shooting gallery, and then he dashed out of the room. A few minutes later, the nurse came in and asked for a specimen.

Within a short time, the verdict came back: I was pregnant, leaving Les and me breathless with joy. To celebrate, I threw up for the gazillionth time, and then I headed home to revamp my life. Les, delighted at the thought of becoming a father again, grinned for months afterward.

We sister chicks are busy about many things. But don't let your Weeble wobble. When life throws you into a spin, enjoy the ride!

*Lord, thank you that, when life takes us for a spin, we can count on you to keep us upright. No matter how dizzy we are or how blurred our vision becomes, you remain steadfast and faithful. Help us to realize those around us are a blend of hard-boiled and delicate and to treat them accordingly. Amen.*

## Cracked-Up Questions

Which egg best describes you: scrambled, hard-cooked, poached, or fried? Why?

Who leaves you spinning?

When was your last hard-boiled response? With whom? Any egg on your face?

List ways you contribute to your world. Then celebrate!

# 30

# Anatomy Class

I was driving down a dirt road at a good clip when I clipped the sideview mirror on the only mailbox on the entire length of the road. The mirror cracked into a hundred pointy shards. The shards didn't fall out of the frame, but they might as well have, since it left me with a distorted view.

Les was impressed that I was able to find the only mailbox in a one-mile area and swipe it. "It's just a gift," I bragged, as I examined my shattered mirror. I could see a dozen reflections of me in those shards . . . all of them broken, which was definitely reminiscent of how I felt about myself most of my life. To tell the truth, those old slivered pictures sometimes still replay inside me, especially when I'm tired, stressed, or feeling like I didn't do something well.

I've wondered where our self-esteem resides. Which body part houses it? Does it bunk in our hearts? Or lease a room in our minds?

I think my esteem might be hunkered down in my stomach. I say that because when I'm feeling fractured, I eat something yummy like strawberry shortcake topped with whipped cream. I feel much better after my indulgence . . . for a while. Those good feelings diminish when I near a scale or when the pleasure of my treat wears off my taste buds. Then I'm back in the kitchen, foraging like a raccoon in the trash.

Now that I think about it, I don't believe esteem lives in my stomach. That's way too acidic; it would have been eaten alive long ago.

Motives trench in the heart, schemes camp out in the mind, but where, oh where, does self-esteem live? Perhaps it's a vagabond or a multitasker and divvies up its locales. Or perhaps it's sharing a room with emotions. It does seem like my emotions feed or starve my self-concept, but I, like you, know that emotions can be unreasonable and often inaccurate; so they really wouldn't make good roommates. But I think they're neighbors who yell back and forth to each other from their front porches.

You don't think self-esteem rents a room from our hormones, do you? Heaven forbid. Why, my hormones are like a popcorn machine, in popping mode most of the time. It might explain why my self-esteem is so riddled and my hormones are so explosive. But, nah, I don't think so. Those two, hormones and self-esteem, would be bad influences on each other.

I wonder if self-esteem is bonded to our eyes? Since esteem is all about our viewpoint of ourselves, that makes sense. Sorta. Except blind people have self-esteem. In fact, my friend Jennifer Rothchild, who is blind, has one of the healthiest self-concepts of anyone I've met. No, it's definitely not the eyes that share quarters with self-esteem.

For sure it's not in our feet. Otherwise, we would be kicking it and stepping on it all of the time. It's not in our hands, or when we felt lousy about ourselves, we would have handed it off to the first person who jogged by. For a moment I considered self-esteem wrapping itself around my backbone for support, but then I remembered the many years I couldn't stand straight because I was so weighed down with self-disgust.

OK, OK, so I failed anatomy class. I give up! I have no idea where my self-esteem lives, but I do know it's alive. Some days, it lags behind what I know to be true; while other days, it inspires me to do cartwheels.

I guess what we should ask ourselves is whether we need to replace the mirror on our self-worth so we can capture a true view of who we are. While I believe we can spend too much time on myopic examinations, I also think we can spend too little effort embracing our value. Before we realize it, that delicate balance slips a notch, which leaves us off kilter. That puts us in as much trouble as viewing ourselves through a fractured mirror, which suggests we are irreparable.

Life comes with distortions—proof the enemy has a strategy, which includes diminishing our view of ourselves so we don't live fully or joyously. Christ has come to heal the network of cracks in our self-esteem, that we might view him more clearly and therefore see our own worth.

*Lord, clear our vision. Prepare us for the inevitable sideswipes of the enemy. Cause us to value ourselves in honorable ways. Amen.*

## Cracked-Up Questions

What cracks your viewing mirror?

How do others' opinions of you
affect how you see yourself?

When did your self-esteem feel sideswiped?

To whom do you feel valuable?

# Part 3

# Going Crackers

*Change, when it comes,*
*cracks everything open.*

—Dorothy Allison

# 31

# Dog Days of Summer

I had just returned from a busy Women of Faith Conference weekend, and I was ready to put my feet up and take a nap. That was when our grand-dog Cody began leaping into the air to announce he wanted to take his walk. This fifteen-pound Jack Russell terrier can leap high with great gusto and look me straight in the eye, making it impossible to ignore him.

Usually, Les puts Cody on a leash, boards his electric cart, and the two of them head out for the walking trails. But on this day, Les had loaned his cart to a friend who had fallen and needed some temporary transportation. That meant I was nominated for the walking honor. Not exactly what I had in mind. I was thinking I needed some physical and emotional restoration. However, a-walking I did go (mumble, grumble).

Cody started out by dragging me down the hill to the path. That jaunt alone felt like it had "chiropractic adjustment" written all over it as I tripped in every yard divot. How a dog that small can pull that hard is beyond me. Soon I realized he was taking me for a jog . . . a rapid one. After he yanked me twenty feet or so, he slowed and began to sniff while I panted until my breathing returned to normal.

At that point, my eyes began to focus on our surroundings. Saucer-sized Queen Anne's lace leaned over the path as if to offer us tea, their tatted wonder shuttered in the gentle breezes. I touched the delicate lace and remembered my childhood socks with lace fringe. Blackberries the size of thimbles glistened in tangles of leaves. Butterflies hung from the vines like petals, their wings pulsating gently, inflating the branches with life.

Slowly, we moved down the path past clumps of black-eyed Susans being serenaded by bumblebees. The drone of their buzz reminded me of a jazz quartet.

When we reached the top of an incline, a sound caught my ear. Much to my delight, it was a brook—a racing, singing, raucous brook that wound its way down the hillside and splashed into a lower pond. Its song was familiar, filled with laughter and joy. Speckled, fat river rocks crowded the brook, adding to its overflowing beauty as the water darted and dashed among them in a lively game of tag.

I was hesitant about leaving the brook, but Cody was sniffing his way into a thicket, and I needed to coax him out. A short way down, day lilies trumpeted, "It's summer; it's summer!" Their yellow, gold, and rust faces reflected in the pond, doubling their fun.

Not far beyond, coneflowers shook their purple petals at the clover below. And a cardinal darted among the foliage like a streak of red ribbon and landed inside an evergreen. High above our heads, a canopy of maples and oaks caused the sunlight to break into a thousand scattered pieces sprinkled across our path.

Cody suddenly sat down, cocked his head, and looked at me. I felt as if he were saying, "See what you almost missed? Why, if it weren't for my insistence, you would be upstairs whining in a chair."

We live in a broken world in which many things are askew; so its no wonder we forget all the lovely things God has written his signature on, starting with the heavens and the earth. How sad for us when we are caught in the tension of our routine and miss the splendor of his creations.

Perhaps because children live so close to the earth, they often are the messengers that remind us of a frog's throaty croak or a cricket's high-pitched chirp or a katydid's tattletale song. Kids are the ones who affirm the dandelion's beauty, a stick's usefulness, and a pebble's colors.

When was the last time you stared into the dazzling pattern of the stars? Or gathered a fistful of lilies of the valley or crammed a jar full of hydrangeas or arranged a vase of peonies? When did you sit at the water's edge and lean in to hear its song? Has it been too long since you sifted sand through your toes or traced the lines on a beautiful shell that you discovered? Who was the last child you introduced to a tadpole? Or helped to catch a turtle?

Creation is bursting with discoveries. A billowing cloud, a sun pattern on a patch of pumpkins, or a bulging garden all comfort us. I guess the Lord knew we would need these undeniable reminders of his presence on earth.

*Lord, for the wonders you have designed that give us pleasure, we thank you. Help us not to miss the glory in a rainbow, the power in a lightning bolt, or the song of a creek. All around us your creativity flourishes. May we be wise enough to rejoice in it. Amen.*

## Cracked-Up Questions

**Who has to nudge you to take a walk?**

**When was the last time you took a leisurely stroll?**

**What did you see?**

**Was the walk rejuvenating? If so, how?**

**What are the songs of summer, autumn, winter, and spring that you hear when you take a walk?**

# 32

# Glass Cracker

My husband is a glass cracker if ever I met one. Les has been breaking glass for years. And, believe it or not, I support his broken behavior.

He's quite deliberate in his crack-and-break method. So much so he even has invested in glass-breaking tools. And when he's done, two things occur: glass shards are scattered hither and yon, and I receive beautiful stained-glass lamps and garden stones. How sweet is that?

Though Les is an excellent glass cracker, he struggles with color selections. Things tend to look either green or brown to him, even when they are red and pink. So I help out. And there are many colors and glass textures to choose from: clear, frosted, wavy, rippled, hammered, pebbled, or very rough. The smorgasbord of colors, textures, and patterns delight an artisan's heart.

I've come to realize, as I've watched Les, that working with stained glass is an art and a craft. It requires a person to have an artistic mind to create the design plus engineering skill to assemble the piece so it's capable of supporting its own weight and surviving the elements.

Most of us think of stained-glass windows as being biblical scenes displayed in churches. Sometimes they depict Christ as a shepherd or angels hovering around the Madonna and Child. But we don't often think about the loss of many of those beautiful, centuries-old windows during World War II.

Bombs shattered so many church windows that the work to repair them brought a renaissance to the art of stained glass. For hundreds of years, design patterns were generally repeated and little innovation occurred. But when those thousands of windows throughout Europe were restored, a renaissance took shape. The ancient art form transformed into a contemporary art form. Rather than creating easily identifiable objects or scenes, these new windows were designed to provide a visual sense of light, color, and even movement. Artists attempted to create a contemplative response from the viewer. Who would think that out of brokenness could come a new movement?

One of my favorite stained-glass pieces Les has made is a floor lamp with more than five hundred pieces that form water lilies. Can you imagine snapping, cutting, breaking, sanding, and soldering that many pieces? Because of Les's dedication to the project, today I have a lovely lamp.

In my cracked-pot existence, I've found that dedication to tedious work is often what it takes to heal from brokenness. It's like fitting pieces into a new pattern of color and light, much like the artists in Europe outfitted churches with new windows through which to contemplate the divine. I've learned not to blanch at the word *tedious*, even though it's a costly process in terms of time and diligence.

Today, as I think about brokenness and the newness that

comes out of it, I can't help but think about the victims of Hurricane Katrina that blasted the Gulf Coast, including Mississippi, Alabama, and Louisiana. Already officials have warned people that it's going to take a lot of time, money, and cooperation to restore their lives to anything resembling normal.

New Orleans experienced not only damage caused by rain and wind, but also from cracks in the levies, which resulted in severe flooding. As I watched the news reports, I wondered what I could do to help. This much I knew: I could give, and I could pray.

On a more personal note, when my life became awash with emotional whirlpools, I remember feeling hopeless. I didn't want to pray; I wanted to be well. But as the waters subsided, I became aware of a lot of debris that needed to be hauled away. I felt like my power lines were down and fear rampaged its windy way through my life, leaving a swath of instability. I could feel my life cracking apart—my emotions were erratic, my relationships were troubling, I was flooded with regret, and my future was dim.

That is, until I committed to rolling up my sleeves and doing the hard work of recovery. That meant I had to institute some changes. It meant I had to own my fears and failures. It meant I had to reestablish myself with others in a healthier way. In other words, I had to begin hauling away the debris of anger and fear, repairing the wind-damaged roof of my mind, and being willing to receive outside rescue assistance from wise counselors when I was in over my head.

Waiting for all the broken pieces of a life to be reworked is neither fast nor easy, but the end result is transformation.

Nothing is more satisfying than to see God's light peering through. It changes everything.

*Lord, thank you for not just instantly fixing us. Thank you that on the long road to recovery, we learn to trust you, we learn of your provisions, and we begin to change and become more like you. When your light streams through our brokenness, suddenly what we had seen as hopeless shards are transformed into a stunning pattern. How fortunate for us; how generous of you. Help us to be lamp stands for your brilliance. Amen.*

## Cracked-Up Questions

**Through what color do you see the world?**

**Why did you choose that color?**

**Define *tedious* with an example from your life.**

**What storms have you lived through?**

**How has God taken the broken pieces of your life and put them together as something beautiful?**

# 33

# Take a Break

On my birthday last year, my friend Debbie Peterson sent me a duck. Yep, a duck. Not a live quacker, but he might as well have been. He's short and squat, which seemed a tad too personal, but my perception changed when I squeezed his wing. He began to sing and dance, and I began to laugh aloud. He was the cutest bundle of yellow, wrapped up in a song. His toe tapped, his wings flapped, and his shoulders (do ducks have shoulders?) gyrated to the song "Singin' in the Rain." He was touting a yellow slicker hat atop his fuzzy head and a green-and-white striped bow around his chubby neck. I'm crazy about this perky bundle of fun because he never fails to make me jiggle with joy.

Ever notice how a good giggle renews your energy and refreshes your attitude? I think that's why comical folks are so popular. Humor makes everyone's life a little easier. Next time you're in a fowl mood, look for a reason to quack up. (I just couldn't resist.)

Sometimes a momentary snicker relieves tension. Recently,

I was seated on a plane, watching other folks as they boarded. A woman who was overloaded with packages was making her way toward the back and didn't realize her purse strap had looped around the arm of a seat as she passed by until it jerked her abruptly to a stop. The man in the seat was trying to unleash it when the woman swung around and saw him tugging on her strap.

Not understanding she had done this to herself, she snapped, "What's wrong with you, mister? Let go of my purse."

The man threw his arms up to indicate he didn't want her purse. That's when she saw the looped strap and realized what had happened. "Oops." She grinned sheepishly. "My fault."

The sweet man smiled. "I couldn't have used it anyway; it doesn't match my shoes." Everyone who saw this drama-turned-comedy tittered in relief.

Humor can cause an enemy to become a friend. And just as this man turned the tone of a potentially unpleasant situation by retaining his humor, we, too, can redirect small calamities into giggle breaks. I'm almost certain everyone in the vicinity of that man wanted to thank him. In fact, the flight attendant did thank him. I'm sure she had seen many similar awkward situations turn unkind. The tight quarters of an airplane amplify unpleasantness or good humor. Instead of internalizing the woman's accusation or being offended by her tone of voice, the man responded with a humorous twist.

Who makes you laugh?

My two grandsons, Justin and Noah, add to the giggles in my life. Recently, my son and daughter-in-law arrived with the boys. Les and I were in the garage talking when they pulled in.

Upon seeing his papa, Noah burst across the garage, yelling all the way, "Papa, Papa!" until he was happily perched in his grandpa's arms. He stroked Les's face repeatedly.

After a few minutes of loving on Les, Noah wanted down. Then at top speed, this towheaded cannonball headed for me. I was now standing in the doorway, so I knelt down to receive my grandson's loving embrace; but Noah came to an abrupt halt just short of my reach. He stated loudly and clearly, "Move!"

"Move?" I questioned.

"Move, Nana!" he repeated. "I wanna see choo-choo." Apparently I was blocking his path to a train we kept at our house for his playtime.

"And what am I, young man—a caboose?"

Noah snickered and then repeated his request: "Move."

Once I moved and recovered from the jolt to my grandma's heart, we all giggled over his antics. There's no doubt who ranks higher at our house. I personally think Les bribes Noah when I'm not looking. In fact, as I'm writing this, I recollect several times I saw Les sneaking him M&Ms. From now on, I'm squealing.

If you haven't been around youngsters recently, take a break and borrow some. Volunteer at a church nursery or a day-care center. They will tickle you. Warning: if you're my age, make sure the kids are returnable.

My friend Marilyn, when feeling unheard in a group, will walk to the nearest wall and begin talking to it. It cracks me up every time. I've taken to imitating Marilyn. I used to take it personally when I tried without success to interject a thought in a multiparty conversation, but not anymore. Now I just release my verbal offering on a nearby door, empty chair, or painting on the wall. Even if no one in my group notices, it makes me chuckle. Of course, be prepared to receive odd stares from passersby.

*Lord, remind us that laughter was your idea and that you highly recommend it for what ails us and for those around us. Help us liberally and appropriately apply this situational salve. Thank you that humor not only can bring relief, but it also can rescue us from behaving unseemly. Amen.*

## Cracked-Up Questions

**Do you dance and sing when folks squeeze your wing? Even if it's raining?**

**When was the last time a child made you laugh?**

**Can you recall a time you were quick to think the worst of another? Why did you respond that way?**

**When did a potential enemy become your friend because of your unexpected response?**

# 34

# Ship Ahoy!

Hope can float a boat. And that's good news. No, make that great news to those of us who have been at the helms of our lives for more than a half century. Wind in our faces, hands on the wheel, eyes on the horizon, we've learned to appreciate any gusts that fill our sails and keep us seaborne.

My sister, Elizabeth, and niece Susan, as youngsters, needed a good gust of wind and a cargo full of hope the day they decided to go boating. My dad owned a small aluminum rowboat that he used to mosey around the lake to "drown worms." The seven-year-old girls never had rowed a boat before, but that didn't stop them from being wide-eyed and willing to take on a new adventure. They conspired not to tell the grownups of their nautical plans, lest those plans be scuttled.

Susan quickly and quietly untied the boat and pushed it away from the dock, while Elizabeth sat poised, like Pocahontas, with oars in hand. Suddenly Susan realized, as the boat drifted beyond her reach, she would be left on dry land if she didn't jump off the dock, swim to Elizabeth, and climb in the boat. Both girls were in over their heads.

Unlike Pocahontas, Elizabeth found paddling cumbersome and uncooperative. She was either swooshing the oars around in midair or cutting so deeply into the lake she couldn't manage the water's weight. In the meantime, Susan couldn't figure out how to hoist herself up and into the skiff. Then, in one fervent last try, Susan's heave-ho tipped the featherlight boat and Elizabeth sideways, causing them both to take on water. The wannabe sailors knew rising water wasn't good, and they shouted their concerns toward dry land.

Hope came in the form of Captain Mom. Mom, hearing distress signals, sprinted toward the waterfront, where she spotted Susan with one leg slung over the sinking boat and Elizabeth, who was in the water by this time, clutching the outstretched oars. Resisting this Kodak opportunity, Mom instead hauled in the waterlogged girls and deposited them safely on shore. Then Mom gave the castaways a reason to remember that occasion for a long time. And it worked. Forty years later, it remains a childhood highlight.

My husband, Les, is still talking about a harrowing ship memory of his own. No wonder. It was his first trip away from home along with hundreds of other young soldiers who were making their way to Europe. Les was accustomed to a rocky ride, having been a commercial fisherman on tumultuous Lake Superior. Yet he still was unprepared for the ocean's fury. Waves pounded the seven-hundred-foot "iron lung," sending all the occupants seeking shelter below. For three days and nights, torrents of sea whipped over the ship stem to stern. No passengers were allowed on deck. Les said they felt like sardines—make that nauseous sardines. Heaving to and fro took on new meaning, and mealtime lost all appeal. (Or should I say, all meals were lost?) The ship had become a reeling sick bay. Yet they were not without hope—hope that the storm would run out of rage, hope that the seaworthy vessel would hold steady on its course, and hope that land was just ahead.

They were grateful when the storm ran out of steam, the vessel remained watertight, and Europe lay straight ahead. After docking, hundreds of weak-kneed, green-at-the-gills soldiers marched down the gangplank and onto solid ground.

I, too, was weak-kneed and green at the gills when my mother died last spring. Waves of grief beat against the hull of my heart at the loss. We had been saying good-bye to her for many years, as she left us a little more every day. Often, I saw it in her eyes, that faraway look . . . like a sea captain entering uncharted waters. And she had a way of talking to herself that made me think she was in conversation with those who had "gone ahead."

Mom's life had spanned many years, and I knew her time to leave was near. But no matter how securely we batten down our emotional hatches, no matter how storm-savvy we might be, no matter how many warnings we receive, nothing prepares us for the tsunami of the death of a parent. The vacancy it leaves in our lives howls like straight-line winds. It wasn't that I couldn't live without her, but I didn't want to. Who would pat my hand and reassure me, make me banana pudding, pray for me with the passion of a parent, listen to my struggles, and put up with me, even when I was unreasonable and cranky?

Yet I found solace in the life preserver of hope, that irrepressible buoy that keeps us afloat. I had hope that this generational waterspout within me would lose intensity, hope that my churning emotions would eventually even out, and hope that Mom's charted course to her "home in Glory" lay ahead for me as well. Until I step onto that shore, I choose to lift anchor and reenter the thrill of the open seas, to risk the exploration of uncharted waters (even if it means getting in over my head), knowing that the final destination will be worth the sometimes-upending voyage.

Recently, I was stopped in my steps by a poster touting these words: "Ships are safe in the harbor, but that's not what ships were built for." Sometimes we don't feel built for storms, but thank God he's in control of us and them.

*Lord, you are our captain and our compass; we can trust you even in uncharted waters. Help us to face the inevitable storms with bravery and humor, knowing you are in control. And when we spring a leak, may we learn to bail without whining. Amen.*

## Cracked-Up Questions

**When did you feel that you were in over your head?**

**Are you safely on shore, or have you jumped off the dock in some area of your life? Explore your answer. Any adjustments necessary?**

**How does hope help our broken hearts?**

# 35

# In a Whirl

My husband bought me a fancy kaleidoscope with a collection of interchangeable wheels. A double wheel is on the front—one wheel is designed to use clear glass shapes, while the other is comprised of colored glass pieces and semiprecious stones. The two wheels give the viewer endless combinations of refracted light.

If my lifestyle allowed, I could sit and spin those wheels for hours. Since that's not practical, I take sneak peeks. The whirl of colors and shapes is magical. And to think, it's just color chips! Yet when they are twirled, they become the bottom of the sea, an upside-down carousel, a rainbow at midnight, a blizzard of confetti, and a rain forest on a sunlit day. There is no end to the fantasy of color.

I also have a wee kaleidoscope that has clear, faceted glass; you see the colors and shapes of whatever you point it toward. At Christmas, I love to aim it at our tree and then spin the tiny tube between my fingers until the view becomes an animation of holiday wonder.

Hope is a type of kaleidoscope. Through its lens, we can believe the impossible and *see* what might be. Hope's hues are rainbow in promise, bringing rays of light into once dark corners. When I think of the colors of hope, I think of Hannah . . .

Hannah was heartsick because she couldn't have a baby. She finally reached the point that she had stopped eating and cried continually. Yet she never gave up hope.

How do I know Hannah still hoped? Because she continued to pray. Oh, I think her hope was wobbly and threadbare and had lost most of its shiny wonder; yet she still beseeched God.

Bearing up under a great disappointment isn't easy, but then add a rival's taunting, and the situation feels heavy beyond bearing. In Hannah's case, her husband's other wife had borne him children. Hannah's emotional pain was so great it almost obscured hope. But Hannah cast herself once again on the altar of God's will and pled her case. She even offered to give her firstborn son to God's service if he would allow her to conceive.

A priest named Eli observed Hannah's radical movements at the altar and thought she was drunk. When he spoke to her, challenging her to reform, she explained her anguish. Eli blessed her and sent her on her way.

After that encounter, something shifted inside Hannah. Someone spun the wheel of her heart, for we are told color returned to her cheeks, she ate, and her face was no longer sad. We don't know how long it was before Hannah gave birth, but Scripture tells us "it came to pass in the process of time that Hannah conceived and bore a son" (1 Samuel 1:20).

Holding on to hope "in the process of time" can be most challenging. I'm sure Hannah experienced moments when she thought she was too broken to be fixed. It seemed that her womb would never open and that she would always be the laughingstock of her wife-in-law (not a term of endearment). Over the years, Hannah must have found the waiting cruel. But after her prayers and her breakthrough moment with Eli, it appears that she was liberated and at peace.

Did God assure Hannah that she would have a child? Or did God assure her that her life was in his hands? Whatever the message, we don't find her agonizing again.

At this point in her story, I hold my breath to see if she will run away with her only child. But Hannah doesn't. She keeps her promise to hand over her son to serve Eli in the temple, and her son Samuel grows up to become a great man of God.

When Hannah offered her son to God, she prayed. This prayer didn't come out of her agony, but out of her victory. Each year, Hannah would return to the temple to the sacrifice of offering, and she would bring Samuel a little robe. Can you imagine the prayers that went into the weaving of that garment?

Eventually, Hannah had a house full of children she had birthed and eyes full of marvel at what God had done. It was as if she were looking through a kaleidoscope. All the things that had seemed so splintered now refracted dazzling light.

*Lord, your plans so exceed our own. Often, we think we have an idea you may have overlooked. Help us to attain a Hannah-level of relinquishment. Wipe our eyes and change our sad countenances to ones of hope. Help us to accept all you offer. "In the process of time," may we not be annoyed by our enemies' taunting but be focused on your multifaceted provisions. Cause our redeemed brokenness to reflect your light. Amen.*

## Cracked-Up Questions

**What color is your future? Why?**

**How have you discovered beauty in your brokenness?**

**What is your greatest disappointment?**

**What has God redeemed for you?**

**What does the term "in the process of time" mean to you?**

## Just for Fun

### Giggle Gauge

My friend Carolyn gave me a magnet for my refrigerator that reads, "There's only one more shopping day until tomorrow."

That made me giggle aloud. I love giggle gifts because a dose of laughter is a gift in and of itself. The magnet business seems to be soaring these days, and I think it's because the makers have discovered the marketability of a good giggle-phrase.

One of my favorites is, "Mom, I'll always love you, but I'll never forgive you for washing my face with spit on your hankie." I howled at that one the first time I saw it because it's so true—we moms do that. My kids didn't see the humor, as they have been the direct recipients of that family cleaning solvent.

I didn't laugh as hard when a friend sent me one that announced, "Be nice to me! With a minimum of effort, I can make things very difficult!" Ouch! Now there's a gal who knows me too well.

Recently, I received a magnet that proclaimed, "If you think you're too small to be effective, you've never been in bed with a mosquito."

What day couldn't use a hearty chuckle? If I can laugh

aloud, I don't even mind that my eyes narrow to slits, leaving me discombobulated.

Have you ever wanted to make your own magnets? I have. Here are the possibilities:

*Menopause: a target for heat-seeking devices*

*Need a facelift? Try smiling!*

*Hormones: emotional chiggers*

*Trifocals: triple ripple*

Well, you can sure tell my age. But since I can't change the modifications or the complications that come with maturing, let me toss back my head and chortle.

How long has it been since you laughed yourself sane? Today, go in search of a giggle—you won't be sorry, no matter your age. And remember to give some giggles to others along the way.

# 36

# Crack the Whip

I love art. Well, not all art. Probably like you, I'm drawn to pieces that ring my chimes.

Winslow Homer is one of my chime ringers. I first spotted one of his prints while eating in a restaurant in my hometown of Brighton, Michigan. Called *The Blue Boat,* the watercolor depicted two fishermen in a rowboat. My dad and my brother were both fishermen, and since both are deceased, you can understand why my heart tugged when I saw the painting. But I also was snagged—hook, line, and sinker—by the blue and green colors.

A year later, I saw a print of a young girl reading a novel; it pleased my eye and captured my interest. The print was entitled *The New Novel.* On a summer's day, the girl was stretched out in the grass, using a knapsack as her pillow. She was lost in the pages of a story—one of my favorite things to do (read, not lay in the grass).

My friend Marilyn had this print hanging in her home, and when I inquired about the artist, I learned it was Winslow

Homer. Once again, his color choices—vivid oranges and contrasting greens this time—pleased my senses.

That second encounter with his offerings set me on a quest to find out more about this artist's work and his life. Since then, my friend Mary has given me two volumes about Winslow (I just love people who know what you want). In them, I learned he was an American artist (1836–1910) who began his career as a draftsman, printmaker, and then an illustrator for *Harper's Weekly*. Homer excelled in composition and detail. He is probably best known for his maritime art, which often depicts fishermen.

I've been a fan of Homer's now for a number of years, and I've seen several of his originals in museums. I've also learned that he was passionate about cooking, flowers, and, of course, the water. I just love knowing he liked the same things I enjoy—even if my culinary skills are iffy. (I'd be better off painting a biscuit than baking one.) Isn't that funny how we love to identify with people? Even those we've only read about.

Another of my favorite Homer paintings is a lineup of boys playing Snap the Whip outside a one-room, red schoolhouse. Why do I like this painting? Certainly the vivid colors, the barefoot boys, and the lush summer day are part of what makes it pleasing to me. But I also like that the painting is filled with contrasts and relationships. You feel the tension as two lads have fallen, while the others remain upright. The boys are playing, yet you are aware their schoolwork awaits them. You see not only human connection but also the jarring disconnection as the two boys tumble helplessly away from the rest.

Isn't that just like life—full of tension? I'm either standing strong and feeling safely connected to others, or I'm thrown headlong, feeling cast aside. And I find that, while I may get to play now and again, work is always close at hand. Yep, I identify with the visual messages of this painting.

One thing I'm certain of. My pleasure in *Snap the Whip* isn't due to my liking the game being played. As a child, I was often a victim of that falderal. Being the runt of the neighborhood, I was the vulnerable tail on the "whip," which meant by the time the swinging momentum made it to me, I was sent skyward, landing about three blocks away. The kids I played Snap the Whip with loved that I was so launchable.

My mom knew how to play Snap the Whip as well. Did I say "play"? Silly me. I meant she cracked the whip. Mom was a lot taller than her height, and she was a no-nonsense lady. She had a great sense of humor, but she expected unmitigated obedience from her children. If she said, "Don't move," trust me, you had better not twitch. Talk about tension.

Mom believed in spankings, and they were usually effective. But on occasion, she would send me out to bring her a switch, which is a very skinny tree limb. Now, honey, those smart. And talk about snapping the whip—that switch could make me boogie. She applied this approach to the lower legs in a back-and-forth movement, causing me to dance, shout, and repent. I can only remember a couple of times that Mom felt inspired to use that type of snappy incentive, but whatever I had done, I didn't do it again.

As an adult, I became a Snap the Whip mom. No, not the kind who used switches (not even once), but the kind who insisted on obedience, especially with my firstborn. Someone once said, "Firstborns should be disposable—for their own protection." It seems our sweet firstborns often reap our inexperience and high expectations. If I could do motherhood over, I'd paint a new canvas . . .

I would say yes more often than I said no.

I'd fly kites instead of flying off the handle.

I'd nuzzle more and nag less.

I'd make dinnertime conversations more like dessert and less like medicine.

I'd applaud small successes with greater enthusiasm.

I'd listen more carefully and lecture less often.

I'd splash in puddles with my children instead of worrying about colds.

I'd giggle more and gripe less.

Discipline would have been more about my child's highest good and less about my fragile disposition.

Then there are times that God "snaps the whip." Actually, Scripture says it this way: "While we were children, our parents did what *seemed* best to them. But God is doing what is best for us, training us to live God's holy best. At the time, discipline isn't much fun. It always feels like it's going against the grain. Later, of course, it pays off handsomely, for it's the well-trained who find themselves mature in their relationship with God" (Hebrews 12:10–11 MSG).

God's loving design is to guide us onto a higher path. It's always for our good. I like that a lot. Guidance that's dispensed for our betterment gives us a sense of security. It helps me not to resist what God is doing in my life, and it reassures me that my difficulties have not launched me outside of his care, even when I feel I've fallen headlong into my muddled circumstances.

*Lord, help us to trust your discipline to accomplish holy purposes. Reassure us again that it is never your intent to hurt us but to help us. And when our connection with others is jarred and broken, may we use that relationship energy to connect even more deeply with you. Amen.*

## Cracked-Up Questions

**Who is your favorite artist? Why?**

**Which artist, entertainer, sports figure, or other celebrity do you identify with? Why?**

**What could you do to make more of a connection with the children in your life?**

**What reminds you that you are safe in God's discipline?**

# 37

# Life in the Valley

In 1893, Katharine Lee Bates traveled by wagon train and mules to the top of Pikes Peak in Colorado. She saw the view from the 14,000-foot pinnacle and was inspired to write "America the Beautiful." Her words are rich with meaning:

> *O beautiful for spacious skies,*
> *For amber waves of grain,*
> *For purple mountains' majesty,*
> *Above the fruited plain.*

While I, too, love the thrill of the mountaintop views, Katharine also reminds me in her stirring song that the fruit grows in the valley. In Scripture, the valley signifies hardship, adversity, fear, difficulty, and even death; while the mountaintops imply conquering, achievement, and victory. Of course, one must approach the high places from the valley floor. So any way we look at it, to experience the heights we must slough through the depths. A valley is a broken place in the landscape—as if it has lost its supports and has sunk down in discouragement. Then, when littered with people, it really looks all cracked up. Yet there are so many fine things about a valley.

For six years, Les and I wintered in a California desert valley. Well, people referred to it as a basin because we were encircled by mountains; but I found that word too, I don't know, bathroomlike. It made it sound like one good flush, and we would all be down the drain. I loved our winter spot, where the mountains greeted us and the sun was out most of the time. And I enjoyed being a valley girl.

I'm not suggesting I want to live in hardship; I don't find brokenness an appealing calling. But as I look back over the years, I can see most of my life has been valley-fied. I've known more daily grind than joy. Yet the joyful times, like the birth of my sons, have been of such intensity that they cast light into the dusty days of drudgery. And joy has a way of reminding us we aren't alone.

I was walking through the kitchen the other night when I noticed Les was watching a National Geographic special on Antarctica. What caught my eye was a father bird ushering his son to the edge of a broken cliff for his first flight, which just happened to be a thousand-foot drop to the ocean below. What a way to break in new wings! The father stayed at his baby's side as he teetered to the edge; and when the baby toppled forth into the air, his dad went with him. What a picture of not being alone!

The father stayed close for the plummeting ride down, down, down until they both sliced into the water, safely bobbing to and fro on the churning sea. It was amazing. Of course, that's easy for me to say—I wasn't the one falling, flailing, and flapping. I wondered if that little bird knew how close his father was to him during his entire descent, ready to swoop under him if he spun out of control. I think baby bird was way too busy trying to survive to look up and see his dad hovering above him. From my high view, the baby was always safe; but his descending perspective was probably very different as he beat his little wings against the enormous sky.

Ever feel that way? As if it's you against the sky? I have. But as my history with the Lord has accumulated into a growing faith, I realize he is with me, ever so close, even as I thrash about in my littleness and my frailty. I'm learning that I can trust his presence, and that realization buoys my spirit, whether I'm on the edge of the ledge, floundering in problems as vast as the sky, or in my splashdown to the valley below.

When the disciples left the valley and joined Jesus on the Mount of Transfiguration, they experienced such a rush of joy that they wanted to stay there. But Jesus let them know they had to go back down, down, down to the people and the problems—because that's where our faith is forged. The valleys are littered with lessons; the wise lean in and learn.

The sights are spectacular from the rocky pinnacles, and we get a great overview of the orchards, but I also want to hold the pear in my hand and taste its sweet offering. That happens in the lowlands. From the peaks, we see the lakes;

but in the valley, we can explore the water's refreshing depths. From the crest, we see the canopy of trees; but in the valley, we can sit in the cool shade and listen as the wind sings through the branches.

We live the majority of our lives in the lowland; yet, if we look close enough, we'll find fruit, catch breezes, and hear music as we learn lessons along the way. For me, that makes the jolts of valley life more bearable and, at times, downright joyful.

*Lord of our valleys, thank you for your guiding presence. And thank you for the bumper crop of blessings amid the low places. Give us eyes not to miss your kind provisions. And when you guide us to the peak, Jesus, may we be as willing to topple off and try our wings as we are to rest on the rocks and enjoy the view. Amen.*

## Cracked-Up Questions

**Define "valley life."**

**What happened when you nudged a "bird" out of its nest—or when you were nudged out?**

**Recall a time when you took a step of faith that required you to "topple forth." How was the landing?**

**Where are you now: on a ledge, flapping in the wind, or bobbing about?**

**Are you too busy surviving to look up? If so, what is one thing you could do immediately to change that?**

**What softens the jolt of the valley for you?**

# 38

# Expect Delays

I was en route to the airport when I spotted a flashing sign. Now, even though this is the same road I always travel and the roads have been under construction for many months, this was the first time I took note of the sign. Flashing in foot-high letters were these words: *Expect delays.*

Isn't that the truth? Everything is at least a little broken. Systems, equipment, people skills, and routines cause holdups, postponements, and big fat delays.

Take grocery carts. I don't know why the one I take is always lame. It clatters so loudly that people stare and snarl at me like it's my fault. In fact, they act as though I brought it from home in this condition just to annoy them. The front wheel keeps jamming, which causes me to belly up to the cart and heave my weight against it just to keep it rolling. Then, when I go around a corner, I have to lift the whole back end (its, not mine) to maneuver around the end displays. What should have taken me fifteen minutes has now taken a chunk out of my morning . . . and I haven't even made it to the checkout line.

*Expect delays.*

Checkout lines were designed to find out if our conversion to Christianity was authentic. There, between the chewing gum and the plastic bags, as we stand next to the conveyor belt, impatience has an opportunity to bloom and flourish. It starts with the person in front of you, who seems to have purposed to pick up every product in the store that isn't priced. And price-check announcements over the PA system seem to be an indicator that all price-check personnel should go on break. By the time the price check is complete and the items are tallied, it now occurs to the purchaser that she actually has to pay for her groceries. That's when she goes in search of checkbooks, credit cards, or money. For women, that means digging into the recesses of their purses. Entire arms disappear into the folds of her bag, wagging about in search of the thirty-two cents it will take to bring financial closure. Fistfuls of debris emerge—gum wrappers, safety pins, and dusty peanuts—until, at last, the rusty coins hinged together with chewed Juicy Fruit are unearthed. By then I have begun to mutter phrases not printed in the New Testament.

*Expect delays.*

Recently, I flew from Detroit to Boston. Direct. What failed to join me was one of my suitcases, which was marked "Priority" by the airlines. How does one suitcase make it, but not the other one? And lucky me, it was the case that contained all my makeup and underwear—which when either are eliminated from my wardrobe causes seismic reactions. Trust me, I need both.

It wasn't like I went to Boston via Okinawa. C'mon, folks,

it was a straight shot. When I reported my missing bag, the lady pushed her computer keys and then announced, "Good news; it's been found in Detroit." To which I quipped, "Well, I hope so, since that's the only place I've been."

*Expect delays.*

When the gentleman put up his hand to stop me from going through security at the airport, I complied. I already had stripped off my shoes, jacket, and purse to be scanned. After an inordinate amount of time, the man waved me through and then immediately began wanding me. The wand sounded like a loaded Geiger counter that had just struck pay dirt as he whisked it around my chubby anatomy. The woman on the scanner then pointed out that my purse and carry-on needed to be searched.

I wondered what about me generated such interest. Was it my intimidating five-foot stature? I don't know, maybe a rash of elderly women had tried to slip their plastic tweezers through, and I fit the MO. Or maybe the security personnel thought it suspicious that I had enough snacks to feed the population of Nebraska.

*Expect delays.*

I bet the Israelites never anticipated that it would take them forty years to reach the Promised Land. Talk about delays. Enemies, rebellion, war, sickness . . . there was always something slowing them down and delaying their arrival.

What looked like sheer inconvenience and man-made barriers actually had been orchestrated by the hand of God. He knew the exact moment they would reach their destination. Delays were as much in his plan as manna and quails.

I remind myself of that when a flight is canceled, a mistake is made, an order is lost, a doctor's report is delayed, or a request is misunderstood. We don't know, but God might be protecting us with these delays. One thing I do know for certain: delays expose human frailty. So maybe we should take notes next time we're held up. It may be God's way of helping us realize our need for trust, patience, adaptability, and relinquishment.

*Expect delays.*

*Lord, thank you for using all things for your purposes. May we not trot past your plan with our frustrations in tow like they are a deserved right. Instead, may we make the best of unexpected circumstances, trusting you to right the wrong, straighten the crooked, find the lost, and repair the broken. Amen.*

## Cracked-Up Questions

**In what ways does your emotional cart wobble?**

**What is the most difficult kind of delay for you?**

**What benefit have you seen in delays?**

**How can God override incompetence?**

## Just for FuN

# Tae Kwon Do

I just came from a tae kwon do class. Nope, I wasn't the student. Are you kidding? I don't think they enlist babes like me . . . you know, the kind with orthopedic underwear.

My five-year-old grandson, Justin, is taking the class, and he's working toward his first belt, which will be yellow. (I have a yellow streak but no yellow belt.) Twelve exceedingly lively boys and one high-kicking girl (yea!) made up the group.

A couple of the benefits of the class are discipline and focus, which makes me think I should take it. (Although I was exhausted when I left the class, and all I had done was watch the students from a distance . . . while seated.) The children had to jump, exercise, kick, count in another language, and yell. Were I to join, I'm almost certain that I would excel at yelling, but I'd need stand-ins for the rest.

I thought it sweet to watch these youngsters follow their leader's instructions. Or should I say, try to follow instructions? The teacher kept raising the bar to retain their attention and challenge their forming abilities. I loved that the instructor, who is a grand master in his field, praised the children not for succeeding but for trying.

The grand master knew that some of what he asked of the children was beyond their capability, but he wanted them to face something formidable. One little boy, who was too small to jump as high as the bar was being held, ducked under it, and the leader congratulated him for doing what he could. He was teaching the lad to face obstacles bigger than he was, even if he approached it differently than others. I liked that.

Hmm, maybe I could take this class, if they let you duck. Although they do want you to kick higher than you're tall. Let's see, I'm five feet. That's sixty inches. Yes, I could do that . . . once.

By the way, I did find out the definition for *tae kwon do*; it means, "Grandma pays."

# 39

# Prevailing Winds

I watched on TV as Floridians nailed windbreakers, in the form of sheets of plywood and strips of aluminum, over their windows to protect their homes from the approaching hurricane. It seems as though Florida has become a breezeway for hurricanes, keeping people on their emotional tiptoes. And while hurricanes aren't new for that area, as of late the frequency and fierceness seems elevated.

I have seasons like that myself. It seems life goes whistling along carefree and comfortable, and then an onslaught of pelting problems comes roaring in. Regardless of my windbreaking efforts, the gale force troubles tug at my tiles and at times even raise my roof. But then, I'm not alone.

Take Daniel, for example. Great guy, holding a good position, suddenly finds himself under a whirlwind of scrutiny and blustery accusations by evil men. Did Daniel deserve their hostility? Nope. But that didn't stop the velocity of the self-serving efforts against him. The next thing Daniel knew, he was locked up with lions. Yes, *lions*—a scary price to pay for praying and living uprightly. Daniel's story would make us wonder what good it does to pray, if it ends with such unfairness. Yet, when we read on, we see that God delivered Daniel from the lion's den without a scratch. Whew. But is that always so? Can we count on God to rescue us out of all our distresses?

Nope again. God often rescues us *in* our distresses, not out of them.

Recently, I saw a report about a man who was accused and convicted of a crime he didn't commit. He was incarcerated for seventeen years before the mistake was rectified. Now, those are hurricane-force winds.

Yet he seemed free of hostility regarding his lost years. How could that be? Well, it turns out he had a windbreaker—gratitude. You can hear it in his words. "I can't allow what I can't change to rob me of the years ahead. I would only add to my years of incarceration if I allowed my heart to be chained with hatred and bitterness. I have every intention of living my liberty."

Wow! And I'm still ticked I didn't have a pony as a kid.

If I'm hearing that man correctly, he's not saying he was grateful for what happened to him, but somewhere along his prison path he learned to be thankful for the good in the midst of reeking injustice. Not an easy lesson.

Ask Joseph. He, too, was unfairly convicted of a crime and spent many years in jail. But when he was released, God had a high position in the Egyptian nation awaiting him. When his brothers (who, out of jealousy, sent Joseph to Egypt to be a slave) found themselves kneeling before him for a handout during a season of famine, Joseph said, "You meant evil against me; but God meant it for good" (Genesis 50:20).

Gratitude requires us to be investigative agents. Joseph sure had to be one to find gratitude when he knew his spiteful brothers had plotted against him. He could have sought revenge, but Joseph knew God had used his hardships for Joseph's own good and for a higher purpose.

It isn't natural to look for good in bad. It's far more human, when bad rears its ugly head, to gaze upon it stymied. But when we believe that God designs and redesigns all things for our good, even when the intent of others is for our demise, it allows us to let them off the hook and look up. Our task is to detect and embrace the good, which means we will have to be alert and discerning if we are to benefit from the windbreaker of gratitude.

I'm not thankful when my heart is broken, yet I'm grateful that through internal ruptures comes a deeper compassion for others who grieve. Our pain causes us to cry out for Christ's ongoing redemptive work within us.

I had no idea how unaware and indifferent I was toward the agony of others until I suffered through a season of intense winds and came out of that time with enhanced sensitivity. It wasn't that I hadn't cared about others; I just didn't have a clue what their struggles were costing them until hardships exacted a high price from me.

Someone once said, "We can only know joy to the degree we have known pain." Hardships have the potential of carving out greater space for God's grace within us. And grace helps us to live with life's inequities without the disabling residuals of anger, bitterness, and disillusionment.

*Lord, you give us strong weather warnings throughout your Word, such as John 16:33: "In the world you will have tribulation." That's clear, not maybe or might, but will. Then you go on to say in the rest of that verse, "But be of good cheer, I have overcome the world." That makes all the difference. That truth has the power to still the storms within us. Forgive our blustering. Regardless of what tumultuous winds bring our way, you are the prevailing one, and we the recipients of good cheer. We acknowledge your constancy and your supremacy. Amen.*

## Cracked-Up Questions

**When were you on your "emotional tiptoes"?**

**Have you ever endured unwarranted hostility? If so, what did you learn about yourself? Others? God?**

**How do people "live their liberty"?**

**Do you think struggle always has benefits? Why?**

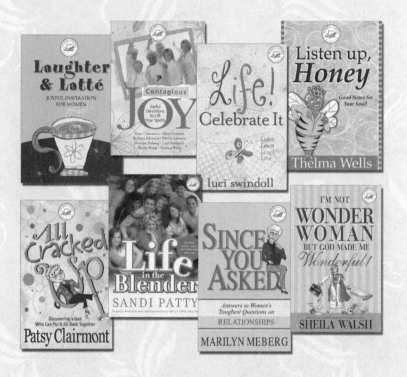

# OTHER SELECTIONS FOR WOMEN OF FAITH

Best-selling authors and Women of Faith speakers, Patsy Clairmont, Mary Graham, Barbara Johnson, Marilyn Meberg, Grammy-award winning singer Sandi Patty, Luci Swindoll, Sheila Walsh, Thelma Wells and dramatist Nicole Johnson bring humor and insight to women's daily lives. Sit back, smile, and enjoy spending some time with these extraordinary women!